HOW TO BE OUTGOING

Step-by-Step Strategies to Transform Your Social Life

Oliver Thrive

Copyright © 2023 by Oliver Thrive

All rights reserved.

No portion of this book may be reproduced in any form without written permission from the publisher or author, except as permitted by U.S. copyright law.

Contents

1. Introduction — 1
2. The Art of First Impressions — 11
3. Mastering Small Talk — 21
4. Building Confidence — 34
5. Expanding Your Social Circle — 43
6. Online Networking and Social Media — 57
7. Overcoming Social Anxiety — 69
8. Hosting and Attending Events — 86
9. Maintaining and Deepening Relationships — 101
10. Conclusion — 117

Chapter One

Introduction

"The only limit to our realization of tomorrow will be our doubts of today." – Franklin D. Roosevelt

In a world that thrives on connections, being outgoing is a superpower that can transform not only your social life but also your entire outlook on the world. Franklin D. Roosevelt's wise words remind us that the doubts we carry today are the only obstacles standing in the way of the limitless possibilities that tomorrow holds. This book, 'How to be Outgoing: Step-by-Step Strategies to Transform Your Social Life,' is your guide to conquering those doubts and unlocking the potential within you.

As you turn the pages of this guide, you'll find practical advice woven into the fabric of personal development. Being outgoing is not a distant goal; it's an achievable reality waiting for you to embrace. Franklin D. Roosevelt's profound insight serves as the guiding star illuminating the path to self-discovery and social mastery.

The doubts that weigh on us today are like clouds blocking the sun of our potential; this book empowers you to clear those clouds. Step into a world where every social interaction becomes an opportunity for growth and connection. 'How to be Outgoing' is more than a book; it's a companion on your journey to becoming the best version of yourself.

Each chapter is a stepping stone, leading you towards a more confident and socially fulfilling life. Unlocking your potential is not a one-time event; it's a continuous process, and this book is your perpetual guide. Social transformation begins with a single step, and this book provides the roadmap for your journey.

Dive into the strategies, anecdotes, and practical tips that will reshape the way you perceive and navigate the social landscape. Franklin D. Roosevelt's words echo through these pages, urging you to cast aside doubts and embrace the boundless possibilities that lie ahead. This book is not just a manual; it's a testament to the transformative power of outgoing behavior.

It invites you to challenge preconceptions, break through barriers, and emerge as a more confident and socially adept individual. The potential within you is a treasure waiting to be unearthed, and this guide is your map to its discovery. With each sentence, you embark on a journey towards a more outgoing, confident, and socially enriched version of yourself.

As you absorb the wisdom within these pages, you'll witness the gradual unfolding of a more socially vibrant and self-assured you. This book is a passport to a world where social interactions become not hurdles but stepping stones to personal growth. The strategies outlined are not just theories; they are practical tools to be wielded in your everyday interactions.

Consider this guide as a conversation with a wise friend, guiding you through the intricacies of social dynamics. The doubts that plague you today will dissolve into opportunities as you immerse yourself in the transformative journey outlined in these pages. This book is a mirror reflecting the untapped potential within you, encouraging you to break free from self-imposed limitations.

Social mastery is not reserved for a select few; it's a skill that can be cultivated and refined, and this book is your training ground. Your social life is not a fixed entity; it's a canvas waiting for the brush strokes of your outgoing and confident self. As you navigate the chapters, you'll find the seeds of confidence and sociability germinating within you.

This book is a lantern illuminating the often overlooked paths to social success and personal fulfillment. The doubts that chain you today will transform into stepping stones propelling you towards a brighter tomorrow. Each sentence is a building block, constructing the foundation of a more socially adept, confident, and outgoing you.

This book is an invitation to rewrite the script of your social life, infusing it with authenticity, confidence, and meaningful connections. Embrace the insights offered here, and watch as your social landscape transforms from a challenge to an adventure. Franklin D. Roosevelt's words act as a catalyst, urging you to shed the doubts that hinder your social growth.

The journey outlined in this book is not just about changing behavior; it's about evolving into a more authentic version of yourself. Social transformation is a journey, and this book equips you with the tools to navigate that journey with confidence and grace. Picture each sentence as a brushstroke on the canvas of your social life, creating a masterpiece of outgoing and vibrant connections.

The doubts addressed here are not insurmountable barriers; they are stepping stones to a more socially confident you. As you absorb the strategies shared in these pages, you'll witness the gradual unfolding of your own social potential. This book is a beacon in the sometimes murky waters of social interaction, guiding you towards clearer and more meaningful connections.

Franklin D. Roosevelt's wisdom acts as a beacon, guiding you away from the shadows of doubt and towards the light of self-discovery. Imagine each sentence as a tool in your social toolkit, each one contributing to the construction of a more outgoing and confident you. Your social life is not predetermined; it's a story waiting for your confident and outgoing narration.

As you internalize the strategies provided, you'll witness a metamorphosis, emerging as a more socially adept and confident individual. This book is a roadmap, guiding you through the twists and turns of the social landscape with poise and confidence. The doubts that echo today will fade into the background as you step into the spotlight of your own social narrative.

Each sentence carries the weight of practical wisdom, offering you the tools to chisel away the doubts that hinder your social growth. This book is a bridge between your current self and the outgoing, confident individual you aspire to become. As you immerse yourself in the strategies shared here, you'll find the contours of a more socially confident you emerging.

Consider each sentence as a note in the symphony of your social transformation, each contributing to the harmonious melody of confident connections. Franklin D. Roosevelt's words are not just an opening statement; they are a call to action, urging you to cast off the doubts that anchor you.

Picture this book as a treasure map, leading you to the hidden gems of social mastery buried within your own potential. As you navigate the chapters, you'll find the knots of doubt unraveling, paving the way for a more socially confident version of yourself. This book is not just a guide; it's a catalyst for change, propelling you towards a more confident and outgoing future.

Understanding Outgoing Behavior

Embarking on this transformative journey, we delve deep into the multifaceted concept of outgoing behavior. Beyond mere sociability, it's a mindset characterized by confidence, curiosity, and authenticity. Throughout, we illuminate the myriad benefits, extending far beyond social settings into every facet of life.

This guide dispels myths and misconceptions, emphasizing that being outgoing is a learnable skill for anyone. It fosters genuine connections, driven by confidence, curiosity, and authenticity. The benefits transcend social circles, influencing personal and professional spheres.

We challenge the misconception that outgoing behavior is exclusive to extroverts. Introverts, too, can develop it to enhance their social experiences. The guide provides tools and strategies, emphasizing authentic self-expression, stepping out of comfort zones, and fostering personal growth.

Being outgoing improves communication skills and meaningful connections. It's about unlocking inherent social potential, leading to more fulfilling lives. The journey involves self-discovery, recognizing strengths, and continuous, gradual effort for skill refinement.

Through diverse perspectives, curiosity prompts connections and experiences, while authenticity fosters genuine relationships. The guide offers practical insights and actionable steps toward cultivating outgoing behavior. It empowers individuals to navigate social interactions confidently, acknowledging the uniqueness of each journey.

Outgoing behavior is inclusive, accommodating diverse backgrounds and perspectives. It's not one-size-fits-all but a customizable skill adapted to individual preferences. It's not just for extroverts; introverts can leverage their strengths authentically.

Understanding outgoing behavior navigates social dynamics, extending benefits to professional settings. It's a catalyst for personal and professional success, prompting self-reflection and celebrating individual strengths. The guide emphasizes meaningful self-expression over constant validation.

Cultural nuances are explored, respecting diverse approaches to social interactions. It's a bridge connecting individuals from different backgrounds, fostering unity and understanding. Practical tools navigate cultural differences, involving small, intentional steps leading to significant transformations.

The journey invites individuals to embrace progress, celebrating successes as milestones. Outgoing behavior is about continuous learning, stepping outside comfort zones, and enhancing social skills without changing core identities. Authenticity is a guiding principle, recognizing unique qualities as strengths.

The dynamic process encourages exploration of diverse social settings, expanding comfort zones gradually. Strategies navigate unfamiliar social territories with confidence and grace, involving making the first move and fostering connections. Nurturing connections and balancing relationships are vital for a harmonious social life.

Online networking is integral, exploring the creation of an engaging profile with authenticity. The guide delves into the nuances of digital communication, offering insights into online etiquette and the balance between virtual and face-to-face interactions.

By the journey's end, individuals hone outgoing behavior skills, equipped to navigate the social tapestry. The guide celebrates individual growth and the potential for a more enriched social life. The journey is ongoing, a transformative path of self-discovery and connection.

Setting the Stage for Transformation

Before we dive into practical strategies for reshaping your social life, let's lay the foundation for transformation. The personal stories shared within these pages illuminate the power of small, incremental steps – the kind that pave the way for monumental shifts. Transformation starts in the mind, and as we guide you through mental preparation, you'll discover that becoming outgoing is an internal shift rooted in self-discovery and acceptance.

As you open yourself to this transformative journey, each personal story becomes a source of inspiration, showing how small steps can set off a ripple effect, reshaping your social landscape. Consider these stories as stepping stones toward a socially enriched life, one deliberate stride at a time.

Within this book, the mosaic of narratives paints a vivid picture, demonstrating the diversity of experiences and revealing that there's no one-size-fits-all approach to becoming more outgoing. These stories are guideposts, forming a pathway toward a socially fulfilling life.

Embedded within personal accounts are echoes of challenges overcome, fears conquered, and resilience born from embracing discomfort. By sharing these stories, our aim is not only to inspire but to underscore the universality of the journey toward outgoing behavior—a journey that transcends age, background, and circumstance.

Transformation may seem like an insurmountable mountain, but these stories reveal that the consistent climb, rather than attempting to conquer the entire peak at once, leads to lasting change. Every individual, regardless of their starting point, can take vital first steps toward a more outgoing and socially vibrant existence.

Consider these narratives guideposts along your journey, pointing the way forward when the path seems unclear or challenging. These shared experiences are not just tales of triumph but also of vulnerability, showcasing that even the most outgoing individuals have faced moments of uncertainty.

The journey toward outgoing behavior is not a linear progression but a series of peaks and valleys, each contributing to personal growth. While your journey may not mirror these stories exactly, within them, you'll find relatable moments resonating with the essence of your unique experience.

Envision these personal stories as lanterns guiding you through dimly lit corridors of transformation. Each small step contributes to a larger transformation, and each personal story contributes to the collective narrative of human connection and shared growth.

Consider these stories as invitations to introspection, encouraging you to reflect on your own experiences, challenges, and triumphs. Through these narratives, you'll come to understand that the journey to becoming more outgoing is not a sprint but a marathon—a gradual, purposeful process of continuous improvement.

These personal stories are the groundwork upon which your own transformation can be constructed, solid and resilient against doubt and hesitation. Just as a single pebble creates ripples, each personal story contributes to the collective impact of this book on your journey to a more socially connected life.

As you delve into these tales, consider them windows into the myriad possibilities that await when you embark on your own expedition toward greater social confidence. The stories shared here are not just narratives; they are invitations to consider, question, and ultimately, redefine your own narrative in the grand story of your life.

As you absorb the lessons embedded in each personal story, you'll find that the path to outgoing behavior is a guided trail, offering insights and wisdom at every turn. The personal narratives are threads weaving the fabric of this guide, creating a tapestry reflecting the diverse, dynamic nature of the journey toward outgoing behavior.

In these stories, you'll discover not only triumphs but also the resilience required to navigate setbacks on the path to becoming more outgoing. These narratives are not just words on a page; they are invitations to join a community of individuals on similar journeys, creating connections beyond the boundaries of the book.

Within each story lies a nugget of wisdom, a lesson learned, or a moment of realization that can serve as a compass as you navigate the terrain of your social transformation. Imagine these personal stories as seeds planted in the fertile soil of your consciousness, ready to germinate into newfound social confidence.

The stories are mirrors reflecting the potential within you, showing that the journey toward outgoing behavior is about unlocking authenticity. These narratives are not just chronicles of change; they are invitations to actively participate in your own narrative, shaping it with intention and purpose.

As you immerse yourself in the narratives, consider them as mentors, offering guidance and encouragement. The personal stories are more than ink on paper; they are living proof that transformation is a tangible, achievable reality.

Picture these stories as bridges connecting you to a community of like-minded individuals, each with their own story to share. In these narratives, you'll find not only relatable struggles but also strategies and insights serving as tools in your own toolkit for social transformation.

The stories serve as reminders that the journey toward outgoing behavior is not about erasing who you are but about revealing and enhancing the authentic self. These personal narratives are a testament to the idea that the journey toward greater social confidence is a universal quest we all share.

Chapter Two

The Art of First Impressions

"You never get a second chance to make a first impression."

Crafting Your Introduction

In the grand theater of life, your introduction is the opening act, setting the tone for your social performance. Picture yourself as the protagonist, the lead character in your social journey. As the curtains rise, consider the profound impact of a simple yet universal language—the power of a smile. It transcends barriers, inviting connection and initiating a dance of shared experiences.

Authenticity is your most potent asset. It's about unveiling the genuine you. Navigate the intricate landscape of body language, guiding you to communicate confidence, approachability, and genuine interest with subtle gestures. Begin with a well-timed smile, recognizing its physiological benefits, from stress reduction to mood enhancement. Explore the art of smiling with your eyes, conveying sincerity and friendliness. Experiment with different smiles tailored to convey a spectrum of emotions. Traverse cultural landscapes, understanding variations in interpreting smiles with cultural sensitivity.

Venture into the orchestration of body language, where each movement is a note in the symphony of communication. Master maintaining eye contact, a powerful tool projecting confidence. Explore mirroring body language to establish connection, open gestures for approachability, and posture for a positive mindset. Delve into the psychology of a firm handshake, understanding its impact on authority and sincerity. Remember, your body language is a dynamic dialogue, leaving an indelible mark on the grand stage of life.

Transition seamlessly into the art of self-introduction, the crescendo of your social symphony. A genuine self-introduction is not a recitation of facts but an invitation for others to connect with the real you. Practice active listening, an essential instrument for meaningful interactions. Tune into the rhythm of conversations, adapting pace and tone for harmonious dialogues. Maintain a positive mindset, radiating optimism during social encounters.

Your energy becomes a guiding force, influencing the overall vibe of interactions. Whether enthusiastic or subtle, the energy you bring shapes the conversation. Genuine interest and curiosity leave a lasting impression. Consider each social encounter as a canvas for mutual growth. Your curiosity becomes a brush, painting vibrant strokes of connection and understanding.

Navigate the intricate dance of small talk, vital for establishing connections. Experiment with various conversational openers tailored to the context. The ebb and flow of dialogue becomes a rhythmic dance, maintaining seamless conversational flow. Maintain a positive and open attitude, acting as a silent conductor directing social interactions toward harmony.

Explore the influence of non-verbal cues—gestures, facial expressions, and proxemics—on social engagement. Subtle nods convey attentiveness, while open gestures signal approachability. Every interaction is a reciprocal exchange. Expressing gratitude fosters positivity and strengthens connections. In this grand performance of your social life, from the initial smile to the final expression of gratitude, each detail contributes to the overall masterpiece.

As you cultivate these skills, your social symphony resonates with authenticity, connection, and the transformative power of genuine human interaction. Step confidently onto the stage of life, not merely as an observer but as an active participant in the vibrant tapestry of human connection.

Dressing for Success

"Dress for success" is not just a cliché; it's a strategic move on the social chessboard. Your attire serves as a silent communicator, expressing volumes before you even speak. In this section, we'll explore the profound impact of your clothing choices on perception, offering insights into selecting the right outfit for various occasions while maintaining a delicate balance between being fashion-forward and authentic.

Your visual language extends beyond colors and patterns; it's a silent dialogue conveying personality, confidence, and attention to detail. Consider the cultural context, and pay attention to accessories, experimenting with textures and fabrics to express your personality in tactile ways.

Pay attention to the fit; it's not just about trends but about clothes that complement your body shape. Footwear, often overlooked, can make a significant impact on your overall look and comfort.

Express your creativity through your wardrobe choices, reflecting your unique self. Wardrobe versatility is key; owning pieces that can be mixed and matched expands your style options.

Dressing appropriately for the occasion demonstrates your respect for the context and those around you. Tailoring your outfit to fit the formality showcases your attention to detail.

Accessorizing strategically transforms a basic outfit into a stylish ensemble. Appreciate the subtle art of layering, creating depth and interest in your overall look. Your wardrobe is an investment; choose quality over quantity for timeless pieces that withstand trends.

Personal grooming is integral; pay attention to hair, nails, and skincare. Understanding color theory guides you in choosing hues that complement your skin tone. Consider the season when selecting your attire; climate-appropriate clothing ensures comfort and practicality.

Embrace the power of accessories as exclamation marks to your fashion statement. Adapt your style to suit your professional environment, showcasing your ability to navigate diverse social settings.

Explore sustainable fashion options to align your wardrobe choices with eco-conscious values. Understanding color psychology empowers you to use colors strategically to convey specific messages. Confidence is your best accessory; wear your outfits with self-assurance and grace.

The concept of a 'capsule wardrobe' encourages simplicity and functionality. Adapt your style to suit your professional environment, showcasing your ability to navigate diverse social settings.

A minimalist approach encourages intentional choices, leading to a clutter-free and stylish wardrobe. Consider the psychological impact of colors when selecting outfits. Experiment with patterns to add visual interest, showcasing your willingness to embrace diversity.

Understand the language of fabrics; choosing the right materials can enhance the comfort and aesthetics of your attire. Pay attention to the details; a well-chosen accessory or a unique pattern can make a significant difference. Develop a signature style that reflects your personality.

Strive for a wardrobe that aligns with your personal values, whether it's sustainability, ethical fashion, or cultural expression. Embrace the joy of experimentation; fashion is an ever-evolving journey of self-discovery and self-expression.

Personal style evolves; don't be afraid to reassess and redefine your wardrobe as you grow and change. Your clothing choices can influence not only how others perceive you but also how you perceive yourself.

Don't underestimate the impact of personal style on your mood and overall sense of well-being. Tailoring your outfit to suit your body shape enhances your natural silhouette, boosting your overall confidence.

Consider the psychological impact of colors when selecting outfits for specific events or meetings. Experimenting with patterns adds visual interest to your outfit, showcasing your willingness to embrace diversity.

Understand the language of fabrics; choosing the right materials can enhance the comfort and aesthetics of your attire. Personal style evolves; don't be afraid to reassess and redefine your wardrobe as you grow and change.

Pay attention to the details; a well-chosen accessory or a unique pattern can make a significant difference. Develop a signature style that reflects your personality and makes you instantly recognizable.

Strive for a wardrobe that aligns with your personal values, whether it's sustainability, ethical fashion, or cultural expression. Embrace the joy of experimentation; fashion is an ever-evolving journey of self-discovery and self-expression.

In embracing these concrete actions and insights, your wardrobe becomes a canvas for self-expression, reflecting your moods, aspirations, and evolving identity. Remember, fashion is not just about clothing; it's a dynamic process that allows you to continually discover and express the ever-evolving you.

Mastering the Handshake

The handshake, a timeless ritual woven into the fabric of human interaction, stands as a testament to the complexities of social finesse. As we embark on a profound exploration of the psychological underpinnings of a good handshake, a rich tapestry of subtle nuances unfolds, transcending it from a mere formality to an art form.

Navigating the diverse tapestry of handshakes isn't just about mastering a social custom but acquiring a universal language of connection. It's a language that communicates openness, understanding, and acknowledgment of shared humanity.

In the corporate world, a firm and confident handshake can speak volumes about your professionalism and competence, setting the tone for a successful collaboration. In personal relationships, it becomes an unspoken vow, a promise of mutual respect and understanding.

The evolution of the handshake mirrors the evolution of societies. In ancient times, it served as a gesture of peace, demonstrating that neither party held weapons. Today, it remains a symbolic gesture of goodwill, a universal acknowledgment that two individuals are meeting on common ground.

Moreover, the handshake is a mirror reflecting the ever-changing dynamics of gender roles. Traditionally, it might have been seen as a masculine expression of strength and dominance, but in the modern era, it has evolved to embrace a more egalitarian perspective.

In the era of globalization, where cultural boundaries blur, the ability to navigate the diverse expressions of handshakes becomes an essential skill. A diplomatic handshake can defuse tension, fostering understanding and cooperation between nations. It becomes a tool for diplomats and leaders to communicate shared goals and aspirations without the need for words.

As you refine your grasp of the handshake's intricacies, consider the variations within a single culture. The way a handshake is executed can vary between generations, regions, and even professions. Understanding these nuances equips you with a versatile tool that adapts to diverse contexts, enhancing your ability to navigate the social landscape.

Delving deeper into the psychology of handshakes, we discover their impact on first impressions. A well-executed handshake can create a positive ripple effect, influencing perceptions of your competence, trustworthiness, and sincerity.

Yet, the handshake is not immune to the winds of change. In an era where physical contact has taken on new significance, navigating the post-pandemic handshake landscape requires adaptability.

The cultural intelligence developed through mastering handshakes extends its influence into broader aspects of cross-cultural communication. It fosters an awareness of diverse communication styles, social norms, and expectations, making you not only socially adept but also culturally fluent.

In a poignant sense, the handshake is a bridge between tradition and modernity, a timeless practice that adapts to the ever-shifting dynamics of human interaction. It is a reminder that as we progress into the future, we carry with us the rich tapestry of customs that have defined us through the ages.

So, embrace the art of the handshake as more than a social grace – consider it a portal into a world of interconnectedness, a tool for navigating the nuances of human connection, and a symbol of your adaptability in an ever-changing world. As you extend your hand in greeting, remember that you are not only engaging in a physical act but participating in a tradition that transcends time, enriching your social journey with every encounter.

Now, let's focus on specific actions and tips to enhance your handshake experience:

1. Perfecting Your Grip:
- Practice a firm but not overpowering grip to convey confidence.
- Adjust your grip based on cultural contexts; some cultures prefer a lighter touch.

2. Duration Matters:
- Aim for a duration that feels natural, avoiding overly prolonged handshakes.
- Be attentive to cues; if the other person initiates a release, follow suit.

3. Cultural Sensitivity:
- Research cultural nuances beforehand, especially in international settings.
- Be open to adapting your handshake style to accommodate diverse cultural practices.

4. Variations within Cultures:
- Acknowledge that even within a single culture, handshake

styles may vary.

- Pay attention to contextual cues, adapting your approach based on the setting.

5. Post-Pandemic Adaptations:
- Understand alternative greetings like elbow bumps, hand waves, or nods.
- Respect personal boundaries, and be open to non-contact greetings if preferred.

6. Non-Verbal Communication:
- Maintain eye contact during the handshake to convey sincerity.
- Ensure a confident posture, standing tall with a friendly facial expression.

7. Adaptability in Professional Settings:
- Gauge the formality of a situation and adjust your handshake accordingly.
- Observe the cultural norms within your industry and adapt your approach.

8. Building on First Impressions:
- Complement your handshake with a warm and genuine smile.
- Follow up the handshake with a concise and memorable self-introduction.

By incorporating these actionable tips into your handshake approach, you'll not only master the social custom but also communicate openness, understanding, and adaptability in various social and cultural contexts.

Chapter Three

Mastering Small Talk

"Small talk is the biggest talk we do." – Susan RoAne

Finding Common Ground

In the intricate dance of human connections, finding common ground emerges as the delicate dance partner, gracefully leading us through the rhythm of shared experiences. The symphony of shared interests orchestrates conversations, seamlessly transforming the often mundane small talk into symphonies of meaningful exchanges that resonate in the hearts of those involved.

Uncover techniques designed to be the compass guiding you toward shared passions—an intricate map highlighting the avenues of connection that traverse the vast landscape of human experience.

1. Map Your Interests:

Immerse yourself in the artistry of steering conversations towards common ground by mapping your own interests. Create a mental inventory of your passions and experiences, ready to share and connect.

2. Active Listening:

Embark on an exploration of the essential skill of active listening. Recognize the subtle nuances of shared interests during conversations. This involves not just hearing but truly understanding the other person's perspective.

3. Diverse Threads:

Explore the rich tapestry of common ground, where diverse experiences interweave to form a beautiful mosaic of human connection. Delve into the psychology of shared passions, unraveling the threads that bind individuals in a shared journey of discovery.

4. Alchemy of Conversation:

Master the art of conversation as a form of alchemy, turning the mundane into the extraordinary through the magic of shared interests. Learn to seamlessly integrate your passions into conversations, creating an atmosphere where connections can naturally evolve.

5. Transformative Power:

Appreciate the transformative power of shared experiences, where seemingly trivial details become the building blocks of lasting connections. Cultivate an awareness of the diversity within shared interests, discovering the beauty in the different hues that compose the collective canvas of humanity.

6. Observation Skills:

Develop a keen sense of observation to identify subtle sparks of commonality, igniting the flames of connection. Embrace the role of shared interests as not only conversation starters but as the foundation upon which genuine relationships are constructed.

7. Online Engagement:

Recognize the universality of shared experiences by transcending cultural and linguistic barriers. Engage in conversations with an open heart, allowing shared interests to serve as the bridge that connects souls in a dance of mutual understanding.

8. Curiosity and Integration:

Cultivate a curiosity about the interests of others, appreciating the uniqueness each individual brings to the mosaic of shared passions. Develop the ability to seamlessly integrate shared interests into conversations, creating an atmosphere where connections can naturally evolve.

9. Reciprocal Exchange:

Understand that common ground is not confined to overt interests; sometimes, it resides in the subtleties and nuances that require a discerning eye. Embrace the reciprocity of shared passions, recognizing that the exchange of ideas and experiences enriches both parties involved.

10. Mindset Shift:

Reframe the notion of small talk as a gateway to profound connections, where shared interests serve as the keys to unlock meaningful dialogues. View shared passions as the language of the heart, transcending the limitations of words and fostering a deep sense of connection.

11. Celebrating Diversity:

Celebrate the diversity within shared interests, appreciating the tapestry of human connection woven with threads of varied experiences. Elevate small talk from a social formality to an art form, where the canvas of conversation is painted with strokes of shared enthusiasms.

12. Rediscover Joy:

Rediscover the joy of discovering common ground, realizing that every shared interest is a treasure waiting to be unearthed in the vast landscape of human connection. Recognize that shared passions are not confined to specific demographics; they are universal threads that bind humanity together.

13. Serendipity in Connection:

Appreciate the serendipity inherent in finding common ground, understanding that it often emerges unexpectedly yet profoundly. Embrace the collaborative nature of shared interests, where individuals contribute their unique perspectives to create a collective masterpiece.

14. Continuous Exploration:

Recognize that the journey of discovering common ground is an ongoing exploration, with each conversation offering new opportunities for connection. View shared interests as the harmonious chords that create a melody of connection, resonating with the shared rhythms of the human experience.

15. Sensitivity to Cues:

Develop a sensitivity to the unspoken cues of shared interests, allowing you to navigate conversations with a sense of intuition and empathy. Understand that shared passions are not confined to formal settings; they can blossom in the most unexpected places, transcending the boundaries of time and place.

16. Inclusive Environment:

Cultivate an environment where shared interests are celebrated, fostering a sense of inclusivity and camaraderie. Recognize the power of shared interests in breaking down barriers, creating a common language that unites individuals from diverse backgrounds.

17. Seeds of Connection:

View shared passions as the seeds of connection, planted in the fertile soil of mutual curiosity and watered by the shared experiences of conversation. Embrace the idea that discovering common ground is not a one-time event but a continuous process of exploration and mutual discovery.

18. Openness to Unexpected:

Develop an openness to the unexpected in conversations, understanding that shared passions can emerge from the most unlikely of sources. Appreciate the interconnectedness of shared interests, where one discovery leads to another, creating a web of connections that spans a lifetime.

19. Collaborative Creations:

View conversations as collaborative creations, with shared interests serving as the raw materials that individuals contribute to the collective masterpiece. Understand that shared passions are not static; they evolve and adapt, providing an ever-changing landscape for meaningful connections.

20. Conversation Starters:

Develop a repertoire of conversation starters that seamlessly integrate shared interests, sparking engaging dialogues from the very beginning. Appreciate the role of shared interests in creating a sense of belonging, where individuals find solace and connection in the shared landscape of interests.

21. Connection Currency:

Recognize that the language of shared interests extends beyond words; it is conveyed through gestures, expressions, and shared moments of understanding. Cultivate a mindset that values shared interests as a form of currency in the economy of human connection, where the exchange is enriching for all parties involved.

22. Generational Bridges:

View conversations as collaborative creations, with shared interests serving as the raw materials that individuals contribute to the collective masterpiece. Understand that shared passions are not confined to a specific age group; they bridge generational gaps, creating connections that transcend time.

23. Dynamic Exploration:

Embrace the idea that discovering common ground is not a one-time event but a continuous process of exploration and mutual discovery. Develop an openness to the unexpected in conversations, understanding that shared passions can emerge from the most unlikely of sources.

24. Web of Connections:

Appreciate the interconnectedness of shared interests, where one discovery leads to another, creating a web of connections that spans a lifetime. Recognize that the pursuit of common ground is an inclusive endeavor, where diverse perspectives converge to create a rich tapestry of understanding.

By incorporating these actions into your interactions, you'll not only find common ground but also cultivate meaningful connections that enrich both your life and the lives of those around you.

Conversation Starters

Breaking the ice in social situations is an art that demands finesse. Craft your introductions with a curated list of conversation openers, transcending generic greetings to unlock more profound connections. Think of each opener as a brushstroke in the masterpiece of your social life, painting vibrant conversations across diverse environments.

Bid farewell to predictable weather talks and embrace openers that catalyze discussions, provoke laughter, and build genuine connections. No longer confined to shallow small talk, use our guidance to dive into engaging conversations that forge bonds beyond the surface.

Imagine yourself armed not just with knowledge but with the skill to effortlessly steer conversations. These openers are invitations to explore common interests, spark laughter, and lay the foundation for lasting connections. Tailor them to different settings and find ease in professional networking events or casual gatherings.

The wisdom in these openers goes beyond words; they guide you to genuine human connection. As you become a conductor orchestrating the symphony of social interaction, understand the alchemy of connection. Each carefully chosen opener is an instrument resonating with authenticity, fostering an environment where meaningful relationships thrive.

In the vast tapestry of human interaction, these openers serve as your palette. Paint conversations that reflect your personality without feeling constrained by social conventions. Armed with confidence, you're not just breaking the ice but melting it, paving the way for warm connections.

Integrate these strategies into your daily interactions for a transformation in how others perceive you and how you perceive yourself. The journey of breaking the ice is an exploration of your capacity for connection and understanding. These openers empower you to initiate conversations with confidence, turning the daunting task of entering a room into an exciting opportunity.

Every word carries resonance, and each conversation opener is an opportunity to leave a lasting impression. Develop an intuition for choosing the right opener for any situation, adapting effortlessly to diverse social environments. The fear of initiating conversations will be replaced with excitement, recognizing the potential within each encounter to create a moment of shared understanding.

In a world filled with noise, the ability to craft meaningful conversations becomes a rare skill. These openers are your ticket to stand out, to be remembered for genuine connections. Tailor them to different settings and navigate social landscapes with ease. The doors opening before you are gateways to a richer, more fulfilling social life.

With these openers, you become a storyteller, weaving narratives that captivate, engage, and leave a lasting impact. Each interaction becomes an opportunity to share a piece of yourself, connecting on a level beyond the superficial. The journey of mastering small talk becomes a journey of self-discovery, uncovering the unique stories that shape your narrative.

The art of conversation is about genuine curiosity and connection. These openers are your compass, guiding you through human interaction with authenticity and empathy. Learn to listen as much as you speak, understanding the flow of a conversation. Awkward silences become opportunities for reflection and understanding.

The beauty of these openers lies in their versatility. They are flexible tools that adapt to the dynamics of each social setting. Navigate professional events, social gatherings, or intimate conversations with ease. Witness the transformation of casual encounters into meaningful dialogues.

In the realm of small talk, every question becomes an invitation, and every answer becomes a bridge. These openers transcend the superficial, inviting others to share their stories. Become a curator of experiences, weaving threads of connection. Awkward silences gracefully transform into opportunities for deeper understanding.

Embrace these openers, and your social landscape will expand with vibrant interactions and diverse connections. The fear of the unknown dissipates, replaced by curiosity for the conversations that await. These openers invite you on a journey of continuous discovery, where each encounter becomes a canvas for exploration and connection.

Consider the journey of mastering small talk not as a destination but as an ongoing exploration of human connection. These openers are your companions, offering guidance, inspiration, and confidence to navigate uncharted territories. Find joy in the unpredictability of conversations, appreciating the diverse stories and perspectives that each individual brings.

With these openers, notice a shift in how you communicate and perceive the world. Initiating conversations becomes an opportunity for growth and self-expression. They are more than words; they are the keys unlocking a world of richer, more meaningful connections. The art of conversation is a journey of continuous transformation, where each encounter becomes a stepping stone towards a more connected and fulfilling social life.

Handling Awkward Silences

Navigating awkward silences is an art that transforms moments of discomfort into opportunities for deeper connections. To gracefully recover from conversational lulls, consider implementing the following strategies:

1. Understand the Ebb and Flow:
- Recognize that pauses are natural and essential for a balanced conversation.

- View awkward silences as opportunities for growth rather than moments to be dreaded.

2. Practice Maintaining Flow:
- Engage in practice exercises designed to effortlessly maintain conversational flow.

- Ensure every pause becomes a launchpad for more engaging discussions.

3. Embrace the Power of Silence:
- Allow silence to create a space for thoughtful reflection.
- Experiment with changing your voice tone during a lull to inject energy and humor.

4. Use Open-Ended Questions and Personal Anecdotes:
- Encourage the other person to share more about themselves with open-ended questions.
- Share a personal anecdote or story to break the silence and create a relaxed atmosphere.

5. Utilize Non-Verbal Cues:
- Use nods and smiles to convey understanding and acceptance.
- Practice active listening by responding genuinely to what the other person is saying.

6. Transitional Phrases and Trivia:
- Use transitional phrases like "Speaking of which..." to smoothly transition between topics.
- Introduce relevant and intriguing trivia or facts to spark new avenues of conversation.

7. Mindful Body Language:
- Maintain open and approachable body language.
- Create a judgment-free environment to encourage the other

person to share their thoughts.

8. Observation and Reflection:
- Use silence as an opportunity to observe surroundings for potential conversation starters.
- Engage in reflective listening, summarizing what the other person has shared to deepen understanding.

9. Facial Expressions and Mirroring:
- Experiment with changes in facial expressions to convey different emotions.
- Employ mirroring techniques to subtly reflect the other person's body language for rapport.

10. Transition and Patience:
- Transition into a related topic by drawing connections between the current subject and a new one.
- Practice patience during silence, allowing the conversation to unfold organically.

11. Metaphors, Analogies, and Playfulness:
- Use metaphors or analogies to add depth to the ongoing dialogue.
- Inject playfulness by introducing a light-hearted question to break the silence.

12. Storytelling and Mindfulness:
- Utilize the art of storytelling to captivate the listener and revive momentum.

- Incorporate elements of mindfulness to guide the conversation to a more present state.

13. Shared Activities and Affirmations:
- Redirect focus by suggesting a shared activity or interest.
- Use affirmations to express understanding and convey that the conversation is valued.

14. Puzzles, Riddles, and Format Changes:
- Playfully challenge with a puzzle or riddle for added fun.
- Suggest a change in conversation format, such as switching from verbal to written communication.

15. Discuss Interests and Passions:
- Discuss shared interests and passions for a foundation of enduring connection.
- Share a compliment or express appreciation for something the other person has said.

16. Mental Preparation and Philosophical Topics:
- Use silence to mentally prepare thoughts for meaningful contributions.
- Introduce a philosophical question or topic to encourage deeper contemplation.

17. Vulnerability and Volume Changes:
- Discuss the power of vulnerability, creating a comfortable environment for sharing.
- Experiment with changes in the volume of your voice to

emphasize certain points.

18. Motivational Quotes and Curiosity:
- Share a motivational or inspirational quote to infuse positivity.

- Express genuine curiosity about the other person's experiences and perspectives.

19. Appreciate the Beauty of Silence:
- Acknowledge the beauty of silence as a canvas for richer, more profound conversations.

- Recognize the potential for connection in each pause, understanding its impact on meaningful dialogue.

Mastering the art of navigating conversational lulls goes beyond avoiding silence; it's about embracing it and transforming it into a tool for connection and understanding.

Chapter Four

Building Confidence

"Confidence is not 'they will like me.' Confidence is 'I'll be fine if they don't'."

Self-Awareness and Acceptance

In the pursuit of transforming into a more outgoing individual, self-awareness serves as the foundational element, the bedrock upon which genuine confidence is constructed. This chapter initiates thoughtfully crafted exercises designed for deep self-reflection, guiding you through the intricate landscape of your personality.

Embark on an introspective journey, unraveling the layers of your identity and acknowledging your unique qualities. These exercises act as a compass, navigating you through the contours of your personality and encouraging you to embrace your distinctive traits with pride.

Confront and challenge the pervasive fear of judgment that often lurks in the shadows of self-doubt. Actively dismantle its power over your self-perception. Genuine confidence blossoms from the fertile ground of self-acceptance – a holistic embrace of oneself, imperfections, and idiosyncrasies included.

The journey through self-awareness is not passive; it's active participation in your evolution—prompt self-discovery, cultivating a profound understanding of your strengths and areas for growth. Examine your beliefs, question assumptions, and celebrate the intricacies that make you an individual.

This is not a one-size-fits-all approach; it's a personalized excavation into the depths of your psyche, uncovering treasures that await acknowledgment and appreciation. The chapter steers you away from self-criticism towards self-compassion, fostering a shift from harsh self-judgment to an empathetic relationship with oneself.

Polish your inner gem, revealing brilliance beneath the surface as you embrace the multifaceted nature of your being. Recognize strengths and befriend vulnerabilities, viewing them not as weaknesses but as opportunities for growth and connection.

Acknowledge the intricate dance between the internal and external worlds. As you become more attuned to your thoughts and feelings, you become more adept at navigating social interactions. Self-awareness is not isolationist but a tool empowering you to engage with the world authentically.

The exercises become stepping stones on your journey to self-empowerment, invitations to experience profound shifts in your perception of self and others. Approach them with an open heart and a curious mind, allowing the process of self-discovery to unfold organically.

The chapter introduces mindfulness practices for being fully present in the moment. True self-awareness extends to a visceral and embodied experience of the present, fostering an appreciation for each moment and the complexity of your emotional landscape.

Addressing the delicate balance between self-reflection and self-acceptance, the journey is about recognizing and embracing the person you are in the present. Be kind to yourself, acknowledging that the path to self-awareness is a continuous evolution, not a destination.

Illuminate the interconnectedness between self-awareness and empathy. As you understand your experiences, cultivate a heightened sensitivity to others. Explore the perspectives of those around you, fostering mutual understanding and compassion. This dual journey of self-discovery and empathy creates ripples of positive influence in the broader social fabric.

The chapter unfolds as a tapestry woven with threads of introspection, acceptance, and growth. Self-awareness is not static but a dynamic, ever-evolving relationship with oneself. The exercises act as catalysts, propelling you forward on your journey of becoming outgoing in a deeply authentic and sustainable way.

Cultivating a Positive Mindset

Confidence is more than a mere external display; it's a mindset that radiates from within. To cultivate this internal strength, let's delve into actionable techniques designed to foster a positive outlook. These strategies are powerful tools to dismantle the barriers erected by negative self-talk, a common hindrance in social interactions.

1. Daily Affirmations:

In your arsenal of self-empowerment, daily affirmations take center stage. These affirmations become the means by which you replace self-doubt with a resilient sense of self-assurance. By adopting a positive mindset, you initiate a transformation that extends beyond personal perception. The world itself undergoes a metamorphosis in its perception of you.

2. Impact on Personal Interactions:

Consistently practicing daily affirmations creates a mental sanctuary where positivity flourishes. This reshapes your internal dialogue and lays the foundation for a more optimistic and empowered version of yourself. The power of positive affirmations lies not only in their ability to reshape your internal dialogue but also in their capacity to act as a magnetic force. They attract opportunities and positive interactions.

3. Positive Thinking as a Catalyst:

In this journey, positive thinking becomes a catalyst for personal growth, propelling you toward a more fulfilling life. Self-reflection becomes a constructive exercise, allowing you to identify and celebrate your strengths. Overcoming negative self-talk involves acknowledging these thoughts and consciously replacing them with affirmations of self-worth.

4. Recognizing and Celebrating Small Victories:

Recognizing and celebrating small victories becomes a customary practice in your newfound journey. Positivity becomes a self-perpetuating cycle, attracting positive experiences. Positive affirmations serve as a compass, guiding you toward a more optimistic and empowered version of yourself. Confidence is not a static state but a dynamic force that evolves with your continuous commitment to self-improvement.

5. Impact on External Judgments:

As you replace self-criticism with self-love, the world responds by reflecting the newfound self-worth you project. Your mindset becomes a key player in shaping the narrative of your life, acting as a resilient shield, and protecting you from the impact of external judgments.

6. Affirmations as Verbal Talismans:

Affirmations act as verbal talismans, warding off negativity and inviting a sense of inner calm. You become a magnet for positivity, attracting individuals who appreciate and resonate with your uplifting energy. The practice of daily affirmations is a commitment to your own well-being and personal growth.

7. Positive Mindset as a Silent Ambassador:

Positivity becomes a self-perpetuating cycle, as your optimistic outlook attracts positive experiences. Affirmations are not just words; they are declarations that shape your reality. A positive mindset is a gift you give yourself, radiating outward and influencing those you encounter. Confidence isn't about perfection; it's about embracing imperfections and seeing them as part of your unique charm.

8. Affirmations as Seeds:

Affirmations are like seeds planted in the garden of your mind, blossoming into a landscape of self-assurance. Positive self-talk becomes a habit, ingrained in your daily routine and influencing your overall well-being. Confidence is a journey, and affirmations are the milestones that mark your progress.

9. Affirmations as a Fuel:

Affirmations are the fuel that propels you forward, igniting the flames of confidence within. A positive mindset doesn't eliminate challenges; it equips you with the strength to face them head-on. Affirmations create a positive feedback loop, reinforcing your belief in your capabilities. Confidence, like a muscle, strengthens with regular exercise, and affirmations serve as the workout routine.

10. Positive Self-Talk as a Shield:

Positive self-talk becomes a shield against external negativity, preserving your inner harmony. Affirmations act as reminders of your inherent worth, prompting you to navigate the world with self-respect. A positive mindset is a beacon of light, illuminating the path toward a brighter and more fulfilling future. Affirmations are the building blocks of self-love, constructing a foundation of confidence within.

11. Confidence as a Contagious Force:

Confidence is contagious; your positive mindset inspires others to embrace their journey toward self-discovery. Affirmations are an investment in yourself, paying dividends in the form of increased self-esteem and resilience. Positive thoughts act as a steady hand, guiding you through the ebbs and flows of life's challenges. Affirmations are the melodies that compose the symphony of self-assurance within your mind.

12. A Positive Mindset as a Gift:

A positive mindset fosters a sense of gratitude, amplifying your appreciation for the richness of life. Affirmations echo in the corridors of your mind, creating an environment where self-belief flourishes. Confidence, when grounded in positivity, becomes an enduring pillar supporting your personal growth. Affirmations are the seeds of change, cultivating a mindset that embraces the transformative power of optimism.

13. Sharing Confidence with the World:

A positive mindset is a gift you share with the world, leaving traces of encouragement in every interaction. Affirmations are the silent cheers that echo within, championing your journey toward self-empowerment. Confidence, rooted in a positive mindset, becomes the cornerstone of a life well-lived.

Public Speaking Basics

Public speaking anxiety, a formidable obstacle on the path to developing outgoing behavior, is a common challenge. This section aims to dismantle this fear with targeted strategies and insights, recognizing that effective communication forms a fundamental pillar of social confidence. To catalyze broader transformations in your social interactions, understanding the intricate connection between communication skills and overall confidence is crucial.

1. Crafting Speeches with Confidence:

Navigating the art of structuring a short speech is pivotal. Through a comprehensive series of practice exercises, we cultivate not only clarity but also conviction and assurance. Tailored exercises address specific aspects of public speaking, including tone, pacing, and body language. Gradually, the once-daunting task evolves into an art you can confidently master, empowering you to express thoughts authentically.

2. Self-Discovery in Speaking Style:

Conquering public speaking anxiety involves self-discovery. Explore your unique speaking style, leveraging strengths and addressing areas for refinement. This introspective journey develops a profound understanding of your voice, fostering self-assurance extending beyond public speaking scenarios. Engage with strategies and exercises to transform fear into a reservoir of potential, unlocking new dimensions of confidence.

3. Challenging Comfort Zones:

Embarking on this journey requires challenging yourself and stepping outside your comfort zone. Provided exercises aim not only to improve speaking abilities but also to reshape your relationship with fear itself. As you engage with these practical activities, a shift in perception occurs – what once felt insurmountable transforms into an opportunity for growth and self-expression.

4. Power of Visualization:

Explore the power of visualization in overcoming anxiety. Through guided exercises, envision successful speaking scenarios to cultivate a positive association with addressing an audience. Visualization becomes a tool not only for reducing anxiety but for instilling confidence carried into real-life speaking engagements.

5. Embracing Vulnerability:

Emphasize the importance of embracing vulnerability. View nervousness as a natural part of the process and learn to navigate these emotions constructively, transforming them into fuel for dynamic and engaging presentations.

6. Audience Engagement:

The concept of audience engagement is woven into the approach. Exercises enhance your ability to read and respond to audience cues, fostering a dynamic and interactive speaking style. Mastering engagement not only captivates listeners but also builds a stronger rapport, boosting confidence in social situations.

7. Non-Verbal Communication:

Delve into the influence of non-verbal communication, from mastering eye contact to understanding gestures and body language. Each nuance is explored to empower you to convey your message authentically, leaving a lasting impression on your audience.

8. Structured Speech and Handling Challenges:

Explore the art of crafting compelling narratives with clear introductions, engaging bodies, and impactful conclusions. Understanding speech structure enhances delivery and provides a solid framework contributing to overall confidence. Techniques to manage unexpected challenges, from technical glitches to impromptu questions, contribute to your effectiveness and resilience as a speaker.

9. Virtual Presentation Skills:

In an era of prevalent digital communication, adapting speaking skills to online platforms is crucial. Practical tips for maintaining engagement, optimizing virtual presence, and utilizing technology become integral components of the discussion.

10. Holistic Approach with Self-Care:

To foster a holistic approach to conquering public speaking anxiety, delve into the role of self-care. Recognize the interconnectedness of mental and physical well-being, and receive guidance on managing stress, cultivating a positive mindset, and maintaining overall health. A resilient and balanced individual is better equipped to face the challenges of public speaking with confidence.

Chapter Five

Expanding Your Social Circle

"Your network is your net worth."

Exploring New Social Settings

Embarking on the journey to become more outgoing involves exploring various social settings, creating fertile ground for personal growth. To start, identify potential arenas for expanding your social horizons, such as joining clubs, attending community events, or participating in group activities. Here are practical steps to ease into these settings and use discomfort as a catalyst for positive change:

1. Research Local Clubs and Interest Groups:
- Explore local clubs or interest groups aligned with your hobbies.

- Attend meetings or events to connect with like-minded individuals.

2. Attend Community Events:
- Participate in community events like fairs or fundraisers.
- Use these opportunities to meet a diverse range of people.

3. Explore Volunteer Opportunities:
- Contribute to a cause while connecting with like-minded individuals.
- Volunteer for events or projects that align with your interests.

4. Join Sports Leagues or Workshops:
- Engage in physical activities by joining a sports league.
- Attend workshops related to your interests for both learning and networking.

5. Utilize Social Media for Local Events:
- Use social media platforms to discover local events.
- Attend meetups focused on specific hobbies to ensure shared interests.

6. Explore Cultural Events:
- Attend art exhibits, performances, or cultural festivals.
- Foster connections with individuals who share an appreciation for the arts.

7. Engage in Group Fitness Classes:
- Foster a sense of community while maintaining a healthy lifestyle.

- Connect with others who share similar fitness goals.

8. Attend Networking Events:
- Expand your professional circle by attending networking events.
- Explore online platforms designed to connect people with similar professional goals.

9. Participate in Community Clean-Up Initiatives:
- Contribute to environmental projects to meet environmentally-conscious individuals.
- Engage in community initiatives that align with your values.

10. Explore Religious or Spiritual Gatherings:
- Connect with individuals who share similar beliefs.
- Attend local cultural festivals to celebrate diversity.

11. Participate in Group Hikes or Nature Outings:
- Combine physical activity with the opportunity to forge new friendships.
- Explore outdoor activities like biking or running groups.

12. Join Gaming or Hobbyist Groups:
- Connect with individuals who share a passion for similar activities.
- Join online forums related to your interests.

13. Attend Social Mixers or Speed Networking Events:
- Facilitate quick and meaningful connections in social set-

tings.

- Investigate local business or entrepreneurship groups.

14. Volunteer for Community Service Projects:
- Contribute your time to meaningful causes and meet like-minded volunteers.
- Explore local farmers' markets to strike up conversations with vendors and visitors.

15. Join Online Gaming Communities:
- Connect with players who share your passion for specific games.
- Explore art classes or workshops, fostering creativity while forming connections.

16. Attend Neighborhood Meetings or Town Hall Events:
- Engage with those in your local community.
- Participate in language exchange programs, connecting with individuals interested in cultural exchange.

17. Attend Mindfulness or Meditation Classes:
- Foster connections with individuals who value mental well-being.
- Engage in charity runs or walks, combining physical activity with social interaction.

18. Explore Local Hobby Shops or Cafes:
- Attend open mic nights or poetry slams.

- Connect with individuals who appreciate creative expression.

19. Explore Historical or Heritage Sites:
- Engage in tours or events to meet fellow history enthusiasts.
- Join gardening clubs or community gardens, fostering connections with plant enthusiasts.

20. Attend Parenting or Family-Oriented Events:
- Connect with others in similar life stages.
- Participate in local photography walks or clubs to connect with visual arts enthusiasts.

21. Explore Social Impact Organizations:
- Engage in initiatives that align with your values.
- Attend cooking classes or culinary events to connect with fellow food enthusiasts.

22. Join Professional Organizations:
- Expand your social circle within your industry.
- Engage in mindfulness retreats or wellness weekends to connect with those interested in holistic well-being.

23. Attend Historical Reenactments or Themed Events:
- Connect with individuals passionate about specific time periods.
- Explore local astronomy clubs or stargazing events, connecting with fellow astronomy enthusiasts.

24. Join Political or Advocacy Groups:
- Connect with individuals passionate about specific causes.
- Attend educational lectures or speaker series, engaging with intellectually curious individuals.

25. Participate in Community-Building Initiatives:
- Contribute to neighborhood gardens or communal spaces.
- Explore local markets or trade fairs to connect with entrepreneurs and small business owners.

26. Attend Local Comedy Clubs or Improve Nights:
- Connect with those who appreciate humor and entertainment.
- Engage in outdoor adventure groups, connecting with individuals who share a love for adrenaline-pumping activities.

27. Seek Mentorship Programs or Groups:
- Connect with experienced individuals in your field or area of interest.
- Explore diverse avenues to expand your social circle, enriching your life with new experiences, perspectives, and lasting connections.

Remember, every new encounter is an opportunity for growth, and the more you embrace the discomfort of the unknown, the more you'll pave the way for positive change in your social life.

Making the First Move

Approaching new people is a crucial skill in expanding your social circle. In these chapters, we'll explore the art of making the first move and provide insights into reading body language cues to gauge receptiveness. Stepping out of your comfort zone holds transformative power, and we'll delve into the nuanced skill of introducing others, fostering connections within your social spheres.

Initiating conversations with strangers, while initially nerve-wracking, is a gateway to new relationships and unforeseen opportunities. Breaking the ice with a genuine smile is a universal invitation, smoothing the approach for both parties. Pay attention to non-verbal cues like open body language; it's a vital indicator of a person's willingness to engage authentically.

Making the first move is about authenticity and a willingness to connect on a human level. Embrace the uncertainty, challenge yourself weekly by initiating conversations with someone new, building the foundation for unwavering confidence. Accept rejection as a natural part of socializing, viewing it as a learning experience rather than a setback.

Experiment with different conversation starters to find what feels authentic for you. People appreciate genuine interest; asking open-ended questions fosters deeper connections. Sharing a personal anecdote or observation creates a relatable atmosphere. Approach social situations with a curiosity mindset, reframing them as opportunities for shared experiences.

Expand your comfort zone by attending events slightly outside your usual scope. Use positive self-talk to reinforce your ability to make the first move and instill a powerful sense of self-confidence. Pay attention to your body language, ensuring it reflects openness. Practice active listening, demonstrating genuine interest in others.

Celebrate small victories in your journey. Making the first move requires adaptation based on context and individuals involved. Experiment with various icebreakers to discover what resonates best with you. Recognize the value of small talk as a stepping stone to deeper connections. Be aware of social cues to understand when a conversation is flowing naturally.

Trust that the more you practice, the more intuitive it will become. View social interactions as opportunities for mutual enrichment. Accept that not every interaction will lead to a lasting connection, but each contributes to your overall social growth.

Develop a repertoire of conversation starters for various settings. Be mindful of the energy you bring; positivity and enthusiasm are contagious. Consider the impact of non-verbal cues, such as eye contact, in building rapport. Approach the first move as an exploration rather than a high-stakes performance.

Reflect on experiences where your initial approach led to meaningful connections. Recognize that making the first move is a skill that evolves with practice. Challenge self-limiting beliefs about your ability to initiate conversations and replace them with empowering affirmations. Experiment with adapting your communication style based on unique personalities.

Use humor to ease tension and create a lighthearted atmosphere. Encourage reciprocal exchange to foster richer connections. Be attuned to verbal cues to gauge comfort and receptiveness. Leverage compliments as a genuine way to create a positive impact. Establish a balance between initiating conversations and allowing space for others to lead.

Embrace the diversity of personalities you encounter. Use open-ended questions to encourage meaningful responses. Practice mindfulness in social situations, staying present and focused. Incorporate elements of active listening to convey genuine interest. Consider the cultural context and adapt your approach to respect diverse norms.

Create a mental toolkit of positive experiences for confidence. Understand that social interactions are dynamic and adapt to the ebb and flow. Develop resilience in the face of challenges, viewing setbacks as opportunities for growth. Encourage yourself to view the first move as an act of generosity. Celebrate your progress, acknowledging strides in becoming more outgoing and building a richer social circle.

Nurturing New Connections

Building and nurturing connections is an ongoing process that extends beyond the initial meeting. Effective follow-up strategies are key; develop a habit of sending personalized emails or messages referencing specific details from previous interactions. Use social media to maintain a consistent presence, sharing valuable resources aligned with their interests. Attend social events together, occasionally surprising them with thoughtful gestures like handwritten notes or small gifts. Collaborate on projects or activities, aligning with shared interests, and schedule regular check-ins to stay informed about important milestones.

Be responsive and timely in your communication, respecting their time. Collaborate on joint projects or attend networking events together, introducing your connections to new contacts. Encourage open communication, plan relaxed social outings, and celebrate achievements together. Actively listen during conversations, offering support during challenging times. Share personal experiences to foster a deeper connection.

Establish a routine for catching up, creating shared traditions or rituals. Attend conferences together to expand your network and introduce connections to each other. Foster inclusivity by connecting with individuals from diverse backgrounds. Plan joint vacations to create lasting memories and build trust. Create a mastermind group for continuous personal and professional growth. Attend educational seminars together, sparking thought-provoking discussions.

Share your network by connecting connections with relevant individuals. Organize themed gatherings, injecting fun into interactions. Encourage pursuits of passion, providing support. Attend cultural events together, broadening perspectives. Celebrate diverse backgrounds within your social circle. Host virtual meet-ups for geographically dispersed connections.

Encourage the exchange of ideas and knowledge within your social circle. Organize skill-sharing sessions, promoting mutual growth. Celebrate successes publicly and share industry insights, fostering a collaborative approach. Create a system for accountability, supporting each other's goals. Attend exhibitions or trade shows together, exploring new opportunities collectively. Engage in joint ventures aligned with collective interests, and plan volunteer activities or charity work, making a positive impact.

Reflect regularly on your social network's growth, adapting strategies for continuous improvement. By incorporating these actions, you'll create a robust social network with enduring relationships. The true magic happens when you invest time, effort, and genuine care into the connections you build.

Remember, building and nurturing connections is not a one-time effort but an ongoing commitment. To further enhance the depth of your relationships, consider the following actionable steps:

1. Customized Engagement Plans: Tailor your approach to each connection by creating personalized engagement plans. Understand their preferences, communication style, and preferred frequency of interaction. This level of customization demonstrates genuine interest and fosters a stronger bond.

2. Shared Learning Initiatives: Collaborate on educational initiatives, such as joint learning sessions or book clubs, to stimulate intellectual conversations. This not only contributes to personal growth but also strengthens the collective knowledge base within your social circle.

3. Interactive Goal-setting: Establish mutual goals and hold each other accountable. Regularly revisit these goals, providing support and encouragement. This shared commitment creates a sense of purpose and cohesion within the group.

4. Strategic Networking Events: Identify and attend networking events strategically. Choose events that align with the collective interests and professional goals of your social circle. This targeted approach ensures that networking efforts contribute meaningfully to everyone involved.

5. Cross-mentorship: Implement a cross-mentorship system where each member of the social circle serves as both a mentor and mentee. This reciprocal exchange of knowledge and guidance strengthens connections by fostering a sense of mutual value and shared growth.

6. Collaborative Projects: Actively seek out opportunities for collaborative projects or ventures that leverage the unique skills and expertise within your social circle. Working together on shared initiatives not only solidifies relationships but also enhances collective achievements.

7. Dynamic Feedback Loops: Establish a culture of constructive feedback within your social circle. Regularly exchange insights on individual and group dynamics, communication styles, and collaborative processes. This openness contributes to continuous improvement and strengthens the overall fabric of your connections.

8. Themed Retreats: Plan themed retreats or getaways that provide dedicated time for bonding and relaxation. These retreats offer a unique environment for deeper connections to flourish, away from the routine of daily life.

9. Cross-cultural Experiences: Explore opportunities for cross-cultural experiences within your social circle. This could involve engaging in activities that expose members to different cultural perspectives, fostering a richer understanding of diversity.

10. Technology Integration: Leverage technology to enhance connectivity. Utilize collaborative platforms, shared calendars, and communication tools to streamline coordination and keep everyone informed and engaged.

11. Storytelling Sessions: Host storytelling sessions where each member shares personal or professional experiences. This practice not only deepens connections by fostering empathy but also provides insights into each other's journeys.

12. Impactful Philanthropy: Channel the collective energy of your social circle into impactful philanthropic activities. Engaging in charitable work together not only makes a positive difference in the community but also strengthens the bonds within the group.

13. Skill Exchange Programs: Implement skill exchange programs where members of your social circle share their expertise with others. This not only promotes skill development but also reinforces the idea that everyone has valuable contributions to offer.

14. Virtual Collaboration Tools: Explore virtual collaboration tools that facilitate seamless interaction, especially for members who may be geographically dispersed. Video conferencing, project management tools, and virtual whiteboards can enhance virtual collaboration.

15. Dynamic Social Media Presence: Maintain a dynamic social media presence collectively. Share achievements, milestones, and insights to showcase the vibrancy and success of your social circle. This not only strengthens existing connections but also attracts potential new members.

16. Periodic Reflection Sessions: Schedule periodic reflection sessions within the group to assess the overall health and dynamics of your social circle. Encourage open dialogue about challenges, successes, and aspirations, fostering a culture of transparency and mutual support.

17. Diversified Networking Strategies: Constantly diversify your networking strategies to adapt to evolving circumstances. This includes exploring new networking platforms, attending different types of events, and experimenting with innovative approaches to connection-building.

18. Ongoing Personal Branding: Encourage members to continuously refine and showcase their personal brands within the group. This could involve sharing professional accomplishments, participating in joint promotional activities, and actively supporting each other's personal branding initiatives.

19. Networking Playbook: Develop a collective networking playbook that compiles successful strategies, lessons learned, and best practices within your social circle. This resource can serve as a guide for both existing members and newcomers, ensuring continuity in your approach to networking.

20. Crisis Support System: Establish a crisis support system within the group where members can turn to each other during challenging times. Whether personal or professional, knowing that there is a reliable support network in place contributes to the overall resilience of the social circle.

Remember, the strength of your social network lies in the shared commitment to growth, collaboration, and genuine connection. Continuously assess and adapt these strategies to suit the evolving needs and aspirations of your dynamic social circle. The true value of your efforts will be evident in the enduring relationships and collective achievements that unfold over time.

Chapter Six

Online Networking and Social Media

"Social media is not just an activity; it is an investment of valuable time and resources."

Creating an Engaging Online Profile

In an interconnected world where digital interactions shape our social landscape, online networking is a powerful tool for connection and growth. Crafting a bio that authentically mirrors your personality is the initial brushstroke on the canvas of your digital presence, a narrative that unfolds in the vast realm of the internet. Selecting profile pictures isn't just about aesthetics; it's about capturing the essence of who you are, and translating your identity into pixels that resonate with authenticity.

Begin by updating your online bio to reflect your true personality. Use genuine language and share aspects of yourself that you're comfortable revealing.

As we delve into the intricacies of online networking, we explore the multifaceted concept of online etiquette. It's more than just a set of rules; it's a code of conduct that underscores the significance of genuine interactions in the digital realm.

Practice online etiquette by actively responding to comments and messages. Engage in conversations with sincerity, fostering connections that go beyond superficial exchanges.

Authenticity becomes the cornerstone, shaping not only how you present yourself but also how you engage with others. Navigating the virtual world demands a level of sincerity that transcends the screen, fostering connections that extend beyond the digital divide.

Reflect on your recent online interactions. Ensure that your responses genuinely reflect your thoughts and feelings, contributing to more authentic digital engagements.

Your online profile, meticulously crafted, metamorphoses into a virtual reflection of your real-world self. It's a dynamic representation, a digital alter ego that captures your interests, achievements, values, and aspirations.

Review your profile pictures. Do they truly represent who you are? Consider updating them to better align with your authentic self.

Each element of your online persona, from the carefully chosen words in your bio to the candid snapshots in your photo gallery, serves as an invitation into your world. It's an invitation for like-minded individuals to connect, for potential collaborators to discover shared interests, and for friendships to bloom in the vast digital ecosystem.

Actively seek out and join online communities that align with your interests. Initiate conversations based on shared passions to foster meaningful connections.

In this era of digital interconnectedness, the value of your online profile extends beyond mere networking; it becomes a testament to your identity, influencing the quality and depth of connections in both the virtual and real realms.

Share a post or update that authentically reflects a recent experience or accomplishment. Invite your network to engage with your genuine self.

In the ever-expanding cosmos of the internet, where virtual threads weave connections between individuals across continents, your online profile is a pixelated fingerprint, contributing to the collective mosaic of digital interactions.

Explore a new digital platform or medium to diversify your online presence. Share your insights or creations in a format that resonates with you, expanding your reach.

Every keystroke, every image carefully curated and shared, adds another layer to the evolving narrative of your digital self. The importance of authenticity in the digital realm cannot be overstated, for it shapes the perceptions of those who encounter your online presence.

Conduct a content audit on your social media profiles. Remove posts or images that no longer align with your authentic self, ensuring your online narrative remains true to who you are.

The art of online networking extends beyond the creation of a static profile; it involves active participation in digital conversations and communities. Engaging in online discussions becomes a dialogue, a two-way street where ideas flow, perspectives collide, and connections emerge.

Join a relevant online discussion or forum. Contribute meaningfully to ongoing conversations, showcasing your expertise and building connections with like-minded individuals.

Balancing the dichotomy between the online and offline realms is essential to navigating the complexities of the interconnected world. While your online profile is a reflection, it is not a substitute for the richness of face-to-face interactions.

Plan an offline meet up or event with individuals from your online network. Strengthen connections by transitioning digital relationships into meaningful in-person interactions.

The digital ecosystem is expansive, encompassing various platforms and mediums. Leveraging these channels strategically amplifies the reach of your digital presence.

Identify a platform or medium that aligns with your goals. Create and share content consistently, establishing yourself as a valuable contributor in your chosen digital space.

As you navigate the digital landscape, remember that online networking is not a one-time endeavor; it's an ongoing journey. Your online profile evolves with each experience, interaction, and chapter of your life.

Set a recurring schedule to update your online profiles. Share regular updates about your professional and personal journey, ensuring your network stays engaged with your evolving narrative.

In this chapter, we embark on a journey through the intricacies of creating a compelling online presence. From understanding the pulse of online etiquette to embracing the dynamics of digital conversations, we equip you with the tools to navigate the interconnected world with authenticity and purpose.

Implement at least one piece of advice from this chapter within the next week. Whether it's updating your bio, engaging in an online discussion, or planning an offline meet up, take a tangible step toward enhancing your online presence.

Your online profile is not just a representation; it's a dynamic force that shapes your digital legacy and influences the connections you forge in the boundless realm of the internet.

Reflect on your long-term goals for online networking. Set specific objectives for your online presence, outlining how you want it to evolve and the impact you aim to make in your digital community.

Engaging in Online Conversations

Navigating the digital realm requires active engagement beyond static profiles. Join relevant online communities aligned with your interests, such as forums or social media groups. Actively participate by sharing insights and experiences, commenting on posts, and engaging in discussions. Explore niche platforms like Reddit for more specialized conversations, making thoughtful contributions within your field.

Diversify your engagement by attending webinars and virtual events, initiating conversations with open-ended questions. Foster a positive online presence through consistent engagement, celebrating both your achievements and those of others. Share valuable resources to contribute to collective knowledge and develop a routine for checking and responding to messages.

Experiment with various content types like infographics, videos, and polls to diversify your engagement. Utilize direct messages for one-on-one conversations with individuals you admire. Maintain professionalism in your tone and language, collaborating on projects with others in your community. Attend virtual meetups and networking events to strengthen connections and humanize your online presence with personal anecdotes.

Offer assistance within your community, staying updated on industry trends, and fostering positivity and inclusivity. Express genuine curiosity in others' perspectives, sharing favorite books or resources to initiate discussions. Participate in challenges or activities across platforms, ensuring a broad and interconnected online presence. Manage your online presence with a strategy, attend virtual conferences to expand your network, and showcase your expertise by answering questions in forums.

Create a professional blog or website to highlight your insights, recognize contributions from others, and respond promptly to comments. Collaborate with influencers or thought leaders for broader impact and share behind-the-scenes glimpses for authenticity. Leverage platforms for skill-sharing, host virtual book clubs, and curate recommended accounts for your followers. Experiment with storytelling techniques and use analytics tools to track your online impact.

Host virtual Q&A sessions, collaborate on joint projects, and create shareable visual content like infographics. Encourage a culture of continuous learning by sharing educational resources and discussing new developments. Implementing these strategies will help build a robust digital presence, cultivating meaningful connections for an enhanced overall social experience.

To further enhance your online engagement and social experience:

1. Promote Skill-Sharing:

Leverage online platforms to offer tutorials or workshops, contributing to your community's growth. Organize or participate in virtual book clubs, fostering intellectual discussions with fellow enthusiasts. Share your expertise to empower others and create a collaborative learning environment.

2. Curate Recommendations:

Create a list of recommended accounts or profiles for your followers to discover new voices and perspectives. Explore emerging social media platforms to stay ahead of trends and connect with early adopters. Engage in cross-promotion with individuals or brands that share common values and interests, expanding your network.

3. Share Behind-the-Scenes:

Provide glimpses into your work or projects, offering an authentic view of your online persona. Collaborate with influencers or thought leaders to broaden your reach and impact. Celebrate your journey and milestones, inspiring others in your online community to pursue their goals.

4. Experiment with Storytelling:

Captivate and resonate with your audience by incorporating storytelling techniques into your online posts. Utilize analytics tools to track the impact and reach of your online engagements. Host virtual Q&A sessions to directly interact with your audience, fostering a sense of connection and community.

5. Collaborate on Joint Projects:

Collaborate on joint projects with members of your online community, fostering a sense of collaboration and unity. Create and share infographics or visual content to convey information in a visually appealing and shareable manner. Utilize polls and surveys to gather feedback from your online community and tailor your content accordingly.

6. Share Inspirational Content:

Share quotes or anecdotes that align with the values and interests of your online audience. Encourage a culture of continuous learning by sharing educational resources and inviting discussions around new developments in your field. Inspire and motivate your community through thoughtful and uplifting content.

By integrating these actionable strategies into your online engagement, you'll not only build a robust digital presence but also cultivate meaningful connections that go beyond mere interactions. Embrace the dynamic nature of the digital realm, staying attuned to the evolving needs and preferences of your online community. As you consistently contribute value and authenticity, your digital presence will become a powerful catalyst for building lasting relationships and enriching your overall social experience.

Digital Networking Strategies

Effectively leveraging social media goes beyond mere networking; it's a transformative tool for personal and career growth. In this digital age, crafting a compelling online persona is crucial. We guide you in creating a dynamic extension of your identity, aligning with your objectives. Delve into online networking intricacies, learning dos and don'ts. Understand digital communication etiquette, fostering meaningful relationships for social and professional growth.

Navigate the digital landscape authentically. Strike a balance between showcasing accomplishments and maintaining a relatable touch. Embrace storytelling, sharing narratives that resonate. Tailor content to reflect professional achievements, personality, hobbies, and passions. Engage in diverse platforms, cultivating an active online presence. Leverage multimedia for engaging formats. Be consistent; maintain a regular posting schedule, balancing self-promotion with genuine interest in others.

Optimize profiles for search engines with relevant keywords. Join online communities, expanding your network. Actively participate in networking events and webinars. Practice digital empathy, fostering respect. Explore virtual mentorship, staying informed about industry trends. Use high-quality visuals, curate and share relevant content, foster genuine connections, and utilize analytics tools for strategy assessment.

Embrace cross-platform promotion, balance personal and professional content. Prioritize quality over quantity. Foster collaboration by engaging in group discussions and contributing to shared initiatives. Encourage user-generated content, seek feedback, acknowledge achievements, and practice digital citizenship. Understand privacy settings, consistently update profiles, and actively participate in joint projects and collaborations.

Seek online testimonials to enhance credibility. Engage in virtual events to expand reach. Craft strategic narratives in online content, consider global reach, and foster community. Monitor online reputation vigilantly, addressing negativity professionally. Strive for authenticity, recognizing its role in building trust and lasting connections.

Continuously refine your online presence to reflect evolving skills, experiences, and accomplishments. Embrace collaborative potential through joint projects, collaborations, and knowledge-sharing initiatives. Seek and provide online testimonials and recommendations to bolster professional credibility.

Participate actively in virtual events and conferences, contributing to panels, discussions, and networking sessions. Master the art of strategic storytelling in your online content, creating narratives that resonate and reinforce your personal brand. Recognize the global reach of social media by engaging with professionals from diverse backgrounds and cultures, broadening your perspective and fostering a sense of community within your online network.

Vigilantly monitor your online reputation, promptly addressing any negative feedback or misconceptions with professionalism. Above all, prioritize authenticity in all your online interactions, understanding that sincerity forms the foundation of trust and enduring connections. In an ever-evolving digital landscape, your thoughtful and strategic approach to social media will not only enhance your personal brand but also contribute meaningfully to your professional journey.

As you navigate the dynamic realm of social media, consider it not just as a platform for self-promotion but as a canvas to showcase your authentic self and build meaningful connections. Remember, the essence of a compelling online presence lies in its ability to convey both professionalism and genuine personality.

To amplify your impact, strategically participate in collaborative efforts within your online communities. Seek out opportunities to contribute to joint projects, engage in shared initiatives, and foster collaborative endeavors. The synergy created through such collaborations not only enhances your visibility but also establishes you as a valuable and engaged member of your digital community.

In the ever-evolving digital landscape, keep a vigilant eye on industry trends and technological advancements. Actively participate in virtual events and conferences, not only to expand your reach but also to stay at the forefront of your field. Your involvement in these platforms not only positions you as an informed professional but also opens doors to new connections and opportunities.

The power of online testimonials and recommendations cannot be overstated. Actively seek them from your network and reciprocate generously. These endorsements serve as a testament to your professional credibility and can significantly influence how others perceive your skills and expertise.

Strive for a delicate balance between personal and professional content. Allow your audience to connect with the person behind the professional facade. Share your experiences, insights, and even occasional glimpses into your personal life. This approach fosters a more human connection, making your online presence relatable and memorable.

Quality should always take precedence over quantity in your online interactions. Each engagement should add value to your network and contribute positively to your online reputation. Foster a collaborative mindset by actively participating in group discussions, offering constructive input, and contributing to shared initiatives. Your willingness to share knowledge and support others strengthens the bonds within your online communities.

Encourage user-generated content within your network. Create a space where others feel empowered to share their thoughts, experiences, and insights. Actively seek feedback on your content, viewing it as a tool for continuous improvement and refinement of your personal brand. Acknowledge and celebrate the achievements of your online connections, fostering a culture of support and encouragement.

Practice digital citizenship by adhering to ethical standards and promoting a positive online environment. Understand the significance of privacy settings, striking a balance between maintaining a professional image and safeguarding personal information. Consistently update your online profiles to reflect your evolving skills, experiences, and accomplishments. Ensure that your digital persona remains current and relevant in the ever-changing landscape of your industry.

In conclusion, as you actively navigate the intricate tapestry of social media, remember that your digital presence is a reflection of your authentic self. By weaving a narrative that combines professionalism with genuine personality, engaging in collaborative efforts, staying informed, and fostering a positive online community, you not only enhance your personal brand but contribute meaningfully to the collective growth of your digital network. Your strategic and thoughtful approach to social media is a powerful tool that can propel you toward continued success in your personal and professional journey.

Chapter Seven

Overcoming Social Anxiety

"Anxiety is a thin stream of fear trickling through the mind. If encouraged, it cuts a channel into which all other thoughts are drained." – Arthur Somers Roche

Understanding Social Anxiety

Social anxiety, a common challenge, often surfaces as an overwhelming fear of judgment or negative evaluation in social situations. To address this, it's crucial to recognize that social anxiety is not a sign of weakness but a genuine hurdle faced by many. Understand that everyone experiences some degree of anxiety, making it a shared human experience.

Physical symptoms like sweating or an increased heart rate are natural responses to stress in social situations. Learn strategies to manage these symptoms effectively. Challenge the misconception that social anxiety only pertains to public speaking; it encompasses various social interactions, from casual conversations to group settings.

Social anxiety often stems from heightened self-awareness and a fear of negative evaluation by others. Counter this by challenging the belief that everyone is constantly scrutinizing your every move in social situations. Individuals with social anxiety may resort to avoidance behaviors, withdrawing from social situations to alleviate discomfort. Accept that overcoming social anxiety is a gradual process requiring self-compassion and consistent effort.

Differentiate between social anxiety and introversion, understanding that introverts may prefer solitude for recharging. Debunk the myth that extroverted individuals are immune to social anxiety. Seeking support from friends, family, or mental health professionals is a strength, not a weakness.

Challenge imposter syndrome that may accompany social anxiety, where individuals feel they don't belong in social settings despite evidence to the contrary. Recognize that social anxiety is not a one-size-fits-all condition, requiring tailored strategies for each person.

Address perfectionism and the fear of making mistakes, common elements of social anxiety, through realistic goal-setting. Embrace self-compassion, understanding that everyone makes mistakes and has moments of awkwardness. Recognize that social anxiety is not a permanent trait; with dedication and practice, individuals can develop more adaptive social behaviors.

Exposure therapy, gradually facing feared social situations, is a proven method for overcoming social anxiety. Understand that social anxiety can impact various areas of life, including work, relationships, and personal fulfillment. With the right support, individuals with social anxiety can cultivate meaningful connections and are not destined for social isolation.

Avoidance behaviors may provide temporary relief but perpetuate the cycle of anxiety in the long run. Recognize that social anxiety may coexist with other mental health conditions, requiring a comprehensive approach to treatment. Reject the belief that using substances like alcohol is a viable solution to cope with social anxiety, as it can exacerbate the problem.

Social anxiety may vary in intensity, from mild discomfort to severe impairment in daily functioning. Acknowledge that mindfulness and relaxation techniques can effectively manage the physical symptoms of social anxiety. Challenge the idea that others' opinions define your self-worth; cultivating a strong sense of self is crucial in overcoming social anxiety.

Recognize that social anxiety may have roots in childhood experiences, and exploring these origins can be a valuable aspect of therapeutic intervention. Debunk the misconception that individuals with social anxiety lack social skills; often, they possess excellent interpersonal skills that may be overshadowed by anxiety.

Realize that social anxiety is not a fixed state; it can fluctuate based on various factors, including stress levels and life transitions. Accept that setbacks are a natural part of the journey to overcoming social anxiety; resilience is built through learning from these experiences.

Understand that the fear of negative evaluation may lead to excessive self-monitoring, creating a cycle of heightened self-consciousness. Challenge the notion that individuals with social anxiety are attention-seeking; often, they prefer blending into the background to avoid scrutiny.

Social anxiety may be exacerbated by societal pressures and unrealistic expectations of social performance. Acknowledge that individuals with social anxiety may excel in one-on-one interactions but struggle in larger groups. Recognize that social anxiety is not solely an individual's responsibility to overcome; a supportive environment plays a crucial role.

Realize that social anxiety is not limited to specific demographics; it can affect individuals of all ages, genders, and backgrounds. Understand that social anxiety may lead to anticipatory anxiety, where individuals worry excessively about upcoming social events.

Challenge the idea that confronting social anxiety requires drastic and immediate changes; small, consistent steps can yield significant progress over time. Recognize that social anxiety may coexist with social media anxiety, where individuals feel pressure to present a curated and flawless version of themselves online.

Acknowledge that self-disclosure and vulnerability can be powerful tools in building connections and alleviating social anxiety. Social anxiety may be fueled by cognitive distortions, such as catastrophizing and mind reading, which can be addressed through cognitive-behavioral techniques.

Challenge the misconception that social anxiety is a sign of incompetence; individuals with social anxiety may excel in their professional and personal lives once their anxiety is addressed. Realize that the fear of embarrassment or humiliation may be a central aspect of social anxiety, leading individuals to avoid social situations altogether.

Acknowledge that social anxiety is not a linear journey; progress may involve setbacks, but each setback is an opportunity for growth. Understand that social anxiety may affect the quality of sleep and overall well-being, emphasizing the importance of holistic self-care.

To effectively combat social anxiety, consider implementing the following practical strategies and actions:

1. Mindfulness Practices:

Engage in mindfulness and relaxation techniques regularly to manage the physical symptoms associated with social anxiety. Incorporate deep-breathing exercises and meditation into your daily routine.

2. Challenging Negative Thoughts:

Identify and challenge cognitive distortions related to social situations. Replace negative thoughts with more realistic and positive affirmations. Cognitive-behavioral therapy (CBT) exercises can be particularly helpful in this regard.

3. Gradual Exposure:

Embrace exposure therapy by gradually facing feared social situations. Start with smaller, less intimidating scenarios, and progressively work your way up to more challenging interactions. Consistent exposure can desensitize your anxiety responses over time.

4. Building a Support System:

Share your experiences and concerns with friends, family, or a mental health professional. Establishing a strong support system can provide reassurance, encouragement, and valuable perspectives on your journey.

5. Holistic Self-Care:

Prioritize overall well-being by focusing on a holistic self-care routine. Ensure you're getting adequate sleep, maintaining a balanced diet, and engaging in regular physical activity. Physical health contributes significantly to mental well-being.

6. Realistic Goal-Setting:

Set realistic and achievable goals for social interactions. Break down larger challenges into smaller, manageable steps. Celebrate each accomplishment, no matter how small, to reinforce positive progress.

7. Self-Compassion Practices:

Cultivate self-compassion by recognizing that everyone makes mistakes and experiences moments of awkwardness. Treat yourself with the same kindness and understanding that you would offer to a friend facing similar challenges.

8. Seeking Professional Guidance:

Consider seeking therapy from a mental health professional experienced in treating social anxiety. Therapeutic interventions, such as CBT, exposure therapy, or acceptance and commitment therapy (ACT), can offer tailored strategies for your specific needs.

9. Exploring Root Causes:

If comfortable, explore potential roots of social anxiety, especially any childhood experiences that may have contributed to its development. Understanding these origins can provide insights for therapeutic interventions.

10. Social Skills Development:

Acknowledge and leverage your existing social skills. Practice one-on-one interactions to build confidence before gradually expanding to larger group settings. Recognize that social skills can vary across different contexts.

11. Self-Disclosure and Vulnerability:

Consider experimenting with self-disclosure and vulnerability in appropriate settings. Sharing personal experiences can deepen connections and alleviate social anxiety by fostering a sense of authenticity.

12. Balancing Social Media Engagement:

Be mindful of your social media use. Acknowledge that curated online presentations may not accurately reflect reality. Limit exposure to social media if it contributes to feelings of inadequacy or heightened social anxiety.

13. Cultivating a Strong Sense of Self:

Challenge the idea that others' opinions define your self-worth. Develop a strong sense of self that is independent of external evaluations. Focus on your values, interests, and strengths to build confidence.

14. Leveraging Cognitive-Behavioral Techniques:

Work with cognitive-behavioral techniques to address specific thought patterns associated with social anxiety. Therapists can guide you through exercises to reshape negative thinking and promote positive behavioral changes.

15. Recognizing Progress and Resilience:

Acknowledge setbacks as natural parts of the journey. Embrace these moments as opportunities for growth and learning. Recognize your resilience in facing challenges and moving forward despite obstacles.

Remember, the journey to overcoming social anxiety is unique to each individual. Consistent effort, self-compassion, and a willingness to seek support can lead to significant progress over time. Each small step you take is a valuable stride towards a more socially fulfilled and confident version of yourself.

Practical Coping Mechanisms

Equip yourself with practical coping mechanisms to navigate social anxiety. Begin by exploring breathing and relaxation techniques that form the foundation for managing anxious thoughts. Experiment with diaphragmatic breathing to regulate your breath, inducing a sense of calm. Introduce progressive muscle relaxation into your routine, systematically tensing and releasing various muscle groups to alleviate physical tension linked to anxiety.

Incorporate aromatherapy into your anxiety management plan using calming scents like lavender or chamomile, known for their soothing effects on the nervous system. Delve into guided visualization exercises to counteract anxious thoughts, transporting your mind to serene settings. Establish a daily mindfulness routine, dedicating a few minutes to mindful breathing and self-awareness. Experiment with meditation techniques, from focused attention to loving-kindness meditation, and practice gratitude journaling to shift your focus away from anxious thoughts.

Craft positive affirmations that reinforce self-worth and confidence. Engage in mindful walking, paying close attention to each step and the sensations in your body. Seamlessly integrate breathing exercises into your daily routine, such as during commuting or waiting in line. Experiment with biofeedback devices like heart rate monitors to gain insight into physiological responses to stress.

Attend mindfulness and meditation classes or workshops for a supportive environment. Join online communities focused on anxiety management to share experiences and learn from others. Create a personalized anxiety toolkit with coping strategies based on the intensity and nature of your anxiety. Identify triggers for social anxiety and develop tailored coping strategies for each specific trigger.

Utilize smartphone apps designed for anxiety management, offering guided exercises and reminders throughout the day. Explore holistic approaches like acupuncture or yoga to complement traditional coping strategies. Engage in mindful eating, savoring each bite and heightening sensory awareness. Experiment with creative expression, such as art or journaling, as a form of therapy to externalize and process anxious thoughts.

Connect with a support system, sharing your journey with trusted friends or family for encouragement. Attend group therapy sessions focused on social anxiety to foster a sense of community. Explore nature as a therapeutic setting, engaging in activities like hiking or spending time in a green space to reduce anxiety. Establish a consistent sleep routine, prioritizing rest for overall mental well-being.

Set realistic and achievable goals, breaking down larger tasks into smaller, manageable steps to reduce anxiety. Practice self-compassion, acknowledging setbacks as a natural part of the journey. Engage in mindful breathing exercises before social situations to center yourself and reduce anticipatory anxiety. Experiment with different forms of physical activity, from yoga to dance, to release tension and promote well-being.

Develop positive affirmations tailored to address specific social anxieties. Attend workshops or seminars on anxiety management to gain insights from experts. Use visualization techniques to create mental images of successful social interactions. Explore aromatherapy by incorporating essential oils known for their calming properties. Journal about anxiety triggers and responses to gain clarity and identify areas for growth.

Cultivate a sense of humor as a coping mechanism, finding lightness in social interactions. Engage in progressive exposure, gradually exposing yourself to social situations to build resilience over time. Attend support groups focused on social anxiety, sharing experiences and coping strategies. Develop a bedtime routine that promotes relaxation, incorporating activities like gentle stretching or reading.

Practice assertiveness training to express needs and boundaries confidently. Incorporate laughter yoga, combining laughter exercises with yogic deep-breathing techniques. Create a visual representation of your anxiety management plan, such as a mind map or vision board, to reinforce your commitment to self-care. Engage in mindful listening during social interactions, fully focusing on the speaker and cultivating genuine connection.

Explore acupuncture for anxiety relief as a complementary therapy. Experiment with alternative therapies like Reiki or crystal healing to discover what resonates with your approach to anxiety management. Attend social events with a trusted friend as a supportive companion, gradually building confidence in social settings. Establish boundaries around social media use to ensure positive contributions to mental well-being.

Engage in sensory-focused activities, such as taking a warm bath or listening to calming music, to create a soothing environment. Practice mindful breathing during moments of social discomfort, using it as an anchor to bring attention back to the present. Celebrate small victories along your journey, recognizing and appreciating progress made in managing social anxiety.

To further enhance your journey in managing social anxiety, consider the following practical steps and actions:

1. Continuously assess and adjust your anxiety management plan. Recognize that strategies may evolve over time, and what worked in the past may need modification. Regularly revisit and refine your toolkit to ensure its relevance to your current needs.

2. Experiment with sensory-focused activities, such as incorporating textures or scents that bring comfort during moments of heightened anxiety. This could involve carrying a small object with a soothing texture or utilizing essential oils known for their calming effects.

3. Incorporate mindfulness into various aspects of your daily routine. Practice mindful showering, paying attention to the sensation of water, or engage in mindful eating by savoring each bite, fostering a heightened awareness of the sensory

experience of food.

4. Explore the benefits of engaging in physical activities that promote well-being and stress reduction. Whether it's through yoga, dance, or other forms of exercise, find a movement practice that resonates with you and integrate it into your routine.

5. Establish a consistent and supportive sleep routine, ensuring that you prioritize sufficient rest. Experiment with activities such as gentle stretching or reading before bedtime to create a calming pre-sleep ritual.

6. Develop assertiveness skills by gradually asserting your needs and boundaries in various social situations. Practice expressing yourself confidently, recognizing that asserting your needs is a fundamental aspect of self-care.

7. Consider the incorporation of laughter yoga into your routine, combining laughter exercises with deep-breathing techniques for a unique and uplifting experience. Laughter has the power to reduce stress and promote a positive outlook.

8. Create a visual representation of your anxiety management plan, such as a mind map or vision board. Visualization can serve as a powerful tool, reinforcing your commitment to self-care and providing a tangible reminder of your progress.

9. Engage in mindful listening during social interactions, not only focusing on spoken words but also tuning into non-verbal cues. Cultivate genuine connections by fully im-

mersing yourself in the present moment during conversations.

10. Explore holistic approaches like acupuncture for anxiety relief. Consult with professionals in the field to determine if these complementary therapies align with your personal approach to anxiety management.

11. Experiment with alternative therapies, such as Reiki or crystal healing, to discover if they resonate with your overall well-being. Be open to exploring diverse methods that complement your existing strategies.

12. Attend social events with a trusted friend as a supportive companion. Having a familiar and understanding presence can provide comfort and gradually build your confidence in navigating social settings.

13. Establish boundaries around social media use to ensure a positive impact on your mental well-being. Evaluate your online interactions and curate your digital space to support your journey in managing social anxiety.

14. Continue to celebrate small victories along your journey, acknowledging and appreciating progress made in handling social anxiety. Cultivate a positive mindset by focusing on your achievements and the growth you experience.

15. Remember that managing social anxiety is an ongoing process, and there is no one-size-fits-all solution. Be patient with yourself, stay committed to your self-care practices, and embrace the continuous evolution of your journey towards

greater social confidence and well-being.

Seeking Professional Help

Seeking professional advice is a crucial step toward growth. Different types of therapy and support, from cognitive-behavioral therapy to support groups, are available. Challenge the stigma associated with seeking help for mental health, realizing it is a sign of strength. Take control of your mental well-being, fostering a holistic approach to personal development that recognizes the interconnectedness of mental, emotional, and physical well-being.

Accept seeking professional advice as an act of self-care. Familiarize yourself with therapeutic approaches, tailoring choices to your unique needs. Cognitive-behavioral therapy provides practical tools for reshaping thought patterns and behaviors. Explore the supportive environment offered by group therapy, recognizing the power of shared experiences in the healing process.

View seeking help as a courageous step toward building resilience. Challenge the stigma around mental health, contributing to a more compassionate society. Recognize that mental well-being is integral to a balanced life. Break down barriers preventing open conversations about mental health, fostering understanding and empathy.

Take pride in prioritizing your mental health, reflecting self-awareness and emotional intelligence. Break down barriers to open conversations about mental health, fostering understanding and empathy. Consider therapy as a proactive step toward enhancing your overall quality of life. Explore therapeutic modalities, recognizing each offers a unique approach to healing and growth.

View therapy as an investment in yourself, acknowledging a healthy mind is essential for a thriving life. Challenge the notion that only "serious" issues warrant therapeutic intervention. Recognize that everyone can benefit from therapy, reframing seeking help as a choice rooted in self-love.

Foster a mindset that views therapy as a tool for self-discovery and personal empowerment. Recognize the strength it takes to confront mental health challenges. Encourage open dialogues about mental health within your social circles, promoting a culture of support and understanding.

Advocate for mental health awareness, dismantling stereotypes that perpetuate shame and silence. Challenge the notion that only severe mental health issues warrant attention. Realize seeking therapy is a commitment to continuous self-improvement.

Understand therapists are trained professionals equipped to guide and support your unique journey. Explore the empowering journey of self-discovery facilitated by therapy. Recognize the transformative potential of therapy in breaking cycles of negative thought patterns and behaviors.

Embrace the community of support available. Acknowledge mental health as a dynamic aspect of your well-being requiring ongoing attention and care. Understand therapy is not a one-size-fits-all solution. Break free from societal pressure, prioritizing your mental health above external judgments.

Recognize strength lies within vulnerability, a force for personal growth. Cultivate a mindset that views therapy as a tool for building emotional resilience. Understand seeking help is an active choice to confront challenges. Embrace the support of a therapist as a valuable resource for navigating life's complexities.

Challenge the notion that seeking therapy is a luxury. View therapy as an opportunity to gain insights into your thought processes, fostering a deeper understanding of yourself. Recognize therapy as a collaborative process promoting a sense of agency. Accept seeking professional advice is a proactive step toward creating positive change in your life.

Embrace the idea that therapy is a gradual and transformative journey toward self-discovery. Recognize seeking professional advice is an act of self-care and a testament to your commitment to personal growth. Foster a holistic approach to personal development that goes beyond societal norms, embracing the interconnectedness of mental, emotional, and physical well-being in your journey.

Embrace the collaborative process of therapy, recognizing it as a partnership between you and your therapist that promotes a sense of agency. Understand that seeking professional advice is not a sign of weakness, but rather, a proactive step toward creating positive change in your life. This acknowledgment is crucial for fostering a holistic approach to personal development that transcends societal norms, emphasizing the interconnectedness of mental, emotional, and physical well-being.

Acknowledge that therapy is not a quick fix but a gradual and transformative journey toward self-discovery. This understanding allows you to appreciate the depth and richness of the therapeutic process. Accepting professional advice becomes an act of self-care and a testament to your commitment to personal growth.

Recognize that the decision to seek help is an active choice to confront challenges and actively work towards solutions. In doing so, you embrace the support of a therapist as a valuable resource for navigating life's complexities. This shift in perspective encourages you to view therapy not merely as a reactive measure but as a proactive tool for building emotional resilience and well-being.

Challenge the societal narrative that perpetuates the misconception that seeking therapy is a luxury reserved for severe issues. Instead, consider therapy an essential aspect of self-care, recognizing its potential to provide insights into your thought processes and foster a deeper understanding of yourself. This mental shift is empowering, allowing you to break free from societal pressures and prioritize your mental health above external judgments.

Understand that therapy offers a personalized and tailored approach to healing and growth. This recognition frees you from the one-size-fits-all expectation and allows you to explore diverse therapeutic options. Embrace the diversity of therapeutic approaches, understanding that what works for one individual may differ for another. Encourage open dialogues about mental health within your social circles, fostering a culture of support and understanding.

Advocate for mental health awareness, actively participating in dismantling stereotypes that perpetuate shame and silence. Challenge the notion that only severe mental health issues warrant attention, acknowledging the spectrum of human experiences. Realize that seeking therapy is not an admission of failure but a commitment to continuous self-improvement.

As you embark on the empowering journey of self-discovery facilitated by therapy, celebrate the transformative potential it holds. Break free from the misconception that seeking help is a solitary endeavor; instead, embrace the community of support available. Recognize that mental health is a dynamic aspect of your overall well-being, requiring ongoing attention and care.

In conclusion, therapy is not just a reactive response but a proactive choice to invest in your mental well-being. It is an opportunity to gain insights, develop emotional resilience, and foster a deeper understanding of yourself. By challenging societal norms and embracing the interconnectedness of mental, emotional, and physical well-being, you actively contribute to your personal growth and well-rounded development.

Chapter Eight

Hosting and Attending Events

"The key to a successful event is to remember that it's all about the guest experience."

Planning Your Event

Transforming your social life is a curated journey that involves more than mere attendance; it's about crafting meaningful experiences. In this chapter, we'll guide you through concrete steps to organize a small gathering that fosters genuine connections.

1. **Selecting the Ideal Venue:**
   - Consider factors like location, accessibility, and ambiance that align with your desired atmosphere.
   - Choose a venue that comfortably accommodates your guest list.

2. **Establishing a Theme:**

- Add a unique touch by establishing a theme, catering to various preferences.

- Themes can range from casual game nights to elegant dinner parties.

3. Paying Attention to Details:
- Enhance the overall atmosphere with thoughtful decorations and lighting.

- Create well-thought-out invitations, setting expectations for the event's style and purpose.

4. Communicating Dress Code and Planning Menu:
- Clearly communicate the dress code to ensure guests feel comfortable and appropriately attired.

- Consider dietary restrictions when planning the menu to offer a variety of food and beverage options.

5. Planning Engaging Activities:
- Foster connections through icebreaker games or discussion topics related to the event theme.

- Arrange seating strategically to facilitate conversation and mingling.

6. Incorporating Music and Capturing Moments:
- Complement the atmosphere with music that enhances the vibrant ambiance.

- Consider hiring a photographer or setting up a photo booth to capture memorable moments.

7. Preparing for Contingencies and Welcoming Guests:
- Have a contingency plan for unforeseen circumstances, such as weather changes for outdoor events.
- Prepare a timeline for the event to ensure a smooth flow of activities and transitions.
- Welcome guests warmly, making them feel appreciated and valued.

8. Fostering Inclusivity and Seeking Feedback:
- Introduce guests to one another and encourage connections to foster inclusivity.
- Capture feedback during and after the event, seeking opportunities for improvement.

9. Expressing Gratitude and Follow-Up:
- Express gratitude to your guests for their presence and participation in your curated experience.
- Follow up with attendees' post-event, expressing appreciation and gathering further insights.

10. Evaluating Success and Sharing Highlights:
- Evaluate the success of the gathering based on the connections formed and the overall atmosphere.
- Share event highlights on social media to extend the positive impact to a broader audience.

11. Using Experience as a Springboard for Future Events:
- Use the experience as a springboard for future events, incor-

porating lessons learned and feedback.

- Collaborate with friends or colleagues to co-host events, expanding the social circle organically.

12. Continuous Refinement of Hosting Skills:

- Continuously refine your hosting skills, viewing each event as an opportunity for personal growth.

- Experiment with different event formats, from intimate dinners to larger social mixers.

13. Exploring Diverse Social Environments:

- Consider organizing events around shared interests or hobbies, creating a sense of community.

- Embrace the unexpected, understanding that spontaneity can add an element of excitement.

14. Staying Updated on Event Planning Trends:

- Stay attuned to emerging trends in event planning, incorporating fresh ideas into your approach.

- Seek inspiration from diverse sources to ensure your events remain dynamic and innovative.

15. Creating Anticipation for Events:

- Create a sense of anticipation for your events by building excitement through engaging invitations.

- Collaborate with local businesses or artisans to add unique elements to your gatherings.

16. Tailoring Events to Seasons and Holidays:

- Tailor events to specific seasons or holidays, injecting a festive and timely atmosphere.

- Encourage guests to provide input on future events, cultivating a sense of shared ownership.

17. Exploring Different Locations:
- Consider hosting events in different locations to explore diverse social environments.

- Foster a sense of community by creating a dedicated space or platform for event attendees to connect.

18. Emphasizing Sustainability in Event Planning:
- Emphasize sustainability in event planning by considering eco-friendly options for decor and catering.

- Create an event playlist that complements the mood, catering to various musical preferences.

19. Celebrating Milestones and Adding Significance:
- Celebrate milestones or achievements during events, adding an extra layer of significance.

- Foster unity among guests by incorporating team-building activities or collaborative projects.

20. Exploring Virtual or Hybrid Event Options:
- Explore virtual or hybrid event options to ensure inclusivity for guests unable to attend in person.

- Reflect on each event as a learning experience, refining your approach based on continuous feedback and personal growth.

By implementing these practical steps, you can curate gatherings that go beyond the ordinary, creating meaningful connections and memorable experiences for yourself and your guests.

Navigating Social Gatherings

Attend social gatherings with the intention of fostering meaningful connections and enriching experiences. Master the etiquette for these events, ensuring you navigate them with poise and observational acumen. Strategies for effective mingling will empower you to engage effortlessly with diverse groups and transition seamlessly between conversations.

Learn the art of gracefully exiting conversations by acknowledging the ebb and flow of social interactions and recognizing subtle cues indicating when to step back naturally. Your ability to navigate events not only enhances your experience but contributes positively to the collective ambiance, fostering a vibrant and enjoyable atmosphere.

Embrace the diversity of social gatherings as a canvas for connecting with individuals from various walks of life. Develop a repertoire of conversation starters suitable for diverse settings. Cultivate an open mindset that encourages inclusivity, making every attendee feel valued and welcome. Experiment with different approaches to mingling.

Practice introducing others, creating connections between individuals who share common interests or goals. Demonstrate tact when joining ongoing conversations and foster curiosity about others by asking open-ended questions that invite deeper discussions. Strive to create a balance between actively participating in conversations and allowing others the space to express themselves.

Encourage a spirit of camaraderie by actively seeking out opportunities to include individuals on the periphery. Navigate social gatherings with intentionality, setting personal goals for meaningful connections and experiences. Exhibit graciousness in both verbal and non-verbal communication. Respect personal space and boundaries, demonstrating sensitivity to individual comfort levels.

Be attuned to cultural nuances, adapting your behavior to ensure inclusivity and cultural sensitivity. Develop exit strategies from conversations that are polite and respectful of others' time. Pace yourself during social events, avoiding the urge to rush through interactions. Utilize social cues, such as eye contact and body language, to gauge receptiveness to continued interaction.

Experiment with icebreaker activities to initiate conversations in a lighthearted manner, fostering an environment of mutual support. Acknowledge and celebrate the achievements and interests of those around you. Learn to handle instances of disagreement with respect and mindfulness. Stay present and engaged in each interaction, recognizing the impact of positive affirmations and compliments.

Foster a collaborative atmosphere by actively participating in group activities or discussions. Exhibit humility by acknowledging and learning from diverse perspectives and experiences. Emphasize the importance of follow-up actions, such as sending thoughtful messages or expressing gratitude, after meaningful interactions.

Encourage others to share their stories, creating a reciprocal exchange of insights and perspectives. Foster a sense of community by recognizing shared values and goals. Demonstrate adaptability by adjusting your communication style to suit the dynamics of different social groups. Recognize that meaningful connections can arise unexpectedly.

Use humor as a tool for connection, lightening the atmosphere and creating moments of shared joy. Embrace the opportunity to learn from diverse backgrounds and experiences. Actively seek opportunities to express gratitude and acknowledge the efforts of event organizers and fellow attendees.

Develop resilience in the face of potential setbacks or awkward moments, recognizing them as opportunities for growth. Demonstrate authenticity by being true to yourself in social interactions, fostering genuine connections based on mutual understanding. Be mindful of your body language, ensuring it aligns with your verbal communication and conveys sincerity.

Recognize the power of vulnerability in forging deep connections. Allow yourself to share genuine thoughts and emotions. Actively contribute to the creation of a positive and inclusive environment by discouraging negative behaviors or gossip. Foster a spirit of collaboration by seeking opportunities to collaborate with others on shared interests or initiatives.

Cultivate a sense of responsibility for the collective well-being of the event. Actively contribute to a positive and respectful atmosphere, celebrating the uniqueness of each individual and appreciating the diversity that enriches the social landscape. Strive to be a source of inspiration, motivating others to embrace opportunities for growth and connection within social gatherings.

Reflect on each social gathering as a chapter in your ongoing journey of personal development. Recognize the continuous evolution of your social skills and connections, understanding that each interaction contributes to the larger narrative of your social journey.

As you embark on this continuous journey of personal development within social gatherings, seize the opportunity to be a source of inspiration for those around you. Motivate others to embrace the inherent opportunities for growth and connection within the dynamics of social events.

Reflect on each social gathering as a chapter in the ongoing narrative of your personal development. Consider the interactions, lessons learned, and the connections forged as integral components of your evolving social journey. Recognize that every encounter contributes to a richer understanding of yourself and others.

In the spirit of ongoing growth, acknowledge the evolving nature of your social skills and connections. Understand that each conversation, each shared moment, contributes to the larger tapestry of your social development. Embrace the fact that growth is not a linear process but a series of interconnected experiences that shape your outlook and interpersonal skills.

As you actively contribute to positive and respectful atmospheres, celebrate the uniqueness of each individual you encounter. Appreciate the diversity that enriches the social landscape, recognizing that every person brings a valuable perspective to the collective tapestry of the event.

Strive to be a beacon of positivity and encouragement, fostering an environment where individuals feel empowered to express themselves authentically. Your genuine interactions, respectful demeanor, and commitment to inclusivity create a ripple effect that positively influences the overall atmosphere of the gathering.

Encourage open dialogue and the sharing of diverse stories and experiences. Foster a sense of community by recognizing shared values and goals that bring individuals together at the event. Actively participate in discussions, embracing the opportunity to learn from the rich tapestry of backgrounds and perspectives present.

Demonstrate adaptability by adjusting your communication style to suit the dynamics of different social groups. Be open to the potential for serendipity in social interactions, recognizing that meaningful connections can arise unexpectedly. Embrace the unpredictability of social encounters as opportunities for spontaneity and personal enrichment.

Use humor as a powerful tool for connection, lightening the atmosphere and creating moments of shared joy. Infuse positivity into your interactions, radiating warmth that uplifts the spirits of those you encounter. Your ability to create an environment of shared joy contributes to the overall vibrancy of the gathering.

Continue to learn from the diverse backgrounds and experiences of those you encounter. Actively seek out opportunities to express gratitude and acknowledge the efforts of event organizers and fellow attendees. Your appreciation for the collaborative effort involved in creating memorable social experiences reinforces a sense of community.

Develop resilience in the face of potential setbacks or awkward moments. View these moments not as obstacles but as valuable opportunities for personal growth. By embracing challenges, you cultivate authenticity and deepen your understanding of both yourself and others.

Be mindful of your body language, ensuring it aligns with your verbal communication and conveys sincerity. The congruence between your words and non-verbal cues enhances the authenticity of your interactions, fostering a deeper connection with those around you.

Recognize the power of vulnerability in forging deep connections. Allow yourself to share genuine thoughts and emotions, creating an atmosphere of authenticity. Your willingness to be open contributes to the creation of a positive and inclusive environment.

Discourage negative behaviors or gossip, actively contributing to a culture of respect and support. Foster a spirit of collaboration by seeking opportunities to collaborate with others on shared interests or initiatives. Cultivate a sense of responsibility for the collective well-being of the event, recognizing that each individual plays a crucial role in shaping the overall atmosphere.

In each social gathering, actively contribute to a positive and respectful atmosphere, celebrating the uniqueness of each individual and appreciating the diversity that enriches the social landscape. Strive to be a source of inspiration, motivating others to embrace opportunities for growth and connection within social gatherings.

As you reflect on each event as a chapter in your ongoing journey of personal development, remember that the evolution of your social skills and connections is a continuous process. Each interaction, whether planned or serendipitous, weaves into the larger tapestry of your social journey, contributing to your growth and enriching the collective experience of those around you.

Following Up Post-Event

The conclusion of an event doesn't mark the end of your social journey; instead, it's a pivotal moment for continued connection and growth. Recognizing the profound impact of thoughtful post-event actions, let's delve into tangible steps to enhance your follow-up skills and foster meaningful relationships.

Crafting Personalized Thank-You Messages:

After an event, seize the opportunity to express genuine appreciation through personalized and impactful thank-you messages. This art of gratitude deepens connections and nurtures a culture of appreciation. Convey your heartfelt sentiments to those who shared the event with you, acknowledging their contribution to the shared experience.

Mastery of the Follow-Up Process:

Understand that mastering the follow-up process is a transformative skill that extends beyond the immediate context. With each post-event interaction, you have the chance to turn a fleeting encounter into a lasting relationship. Delve into the intricacies of expressing gratitude to solidify your presence within your social circles.

Embrace the Ripple Effect:

Recognize the ripple effect that emanates from your post-event engagements. The positive energy and goodwill you generate have the power to shape the dynamics of your social landscape. As you navigate the post-event phase, appreciate the threads of continuity it weaves, reinforcing the bonds forged during shared experiences.

Reciprocity and Building Trust:

Discover the beauty of reciprocity in the post-event landscape. Your genuine efforts to connect inspire others to reciprocate, creating a harmonious and interconnected social ecosystem. Each thank-you message becomes a building block, constructing a foundation of trust and goodwill that supports lasting relationships.

Investment in Longevity:

Explore the profound impact of timely and sincere follow-ups. The effort invested in post-event interactions is an investment in the longevity of your social connections. Consistently engaging with others after events contributes to the resilience of your social fabric, strengthening ties within a diverse and vibrant community.

Expressing Gratitude as a Reciprocal Exchange:

Uncover the joy in the process of expressing gratitude, understanding that the act of appreciation is a reciprocal exchange that enriches both the giver and the receiver. Each follow-up action becomes a brushstroke on the canvas of your social portrait, contributing to the masterpiece of interconnected lives.

Garden of Connection:

Consider the post-event phase as a garden where seeds of connection are sown, tended with care, and eventually blossom into flourishing friendships and collaborations. The art of crafting thank-you messages becomes a tool of emotional intelligence, allowing you to communicate gratitude and a genuine understanding of shared experiences.

Contribution to a Social Ecosystem:

Through meticulous post-event engagement, you contribute to the creation of a social ecosystem characterized by reciprocity, mutual support, and shared moments of joy. Understand the enduring impact of your interactions as the positivity you instill continues to resonate and reverberate within your social circles.

Deepening Relationships:

Appreciate the depth of post-event connections, recognizing that they are not merely superficial exchanges but stepping stones towards profound and lasting relationships. Navigate the post-event landscape with intention, viewing each follow-up action as a conscious investment in the relational wealth of your social network.

Pillar Within Your Social Circles:

Mastering the art of post-event interactions positions you as a pillar within your social circles. Offer support, encouragement, and a genuine commitment to the well-being of those around you. Recognize the post-event phase as a canvas where you have the opportunity to paint vivid strokes of connection, transforming transient encounters into enduring relationships.

Immersing in Richness:

Immerse yourself in the richness of post-event interactions, discovering the reciprocity that blossoms when you invest time and energy in expressing gratitude and cultivating meaningful connections. Embrace the philosophy that the conclusion of an event is not an endpoint but a gateway to deeper understanding, collaboration, and the shared tapestry of human experience.

As you embark on the journey of post-event engagement, unveil the potential for personal and collective growth. Understand that the bonds you nurture extend beyond the immediate horizon of the event itself. By mastering the art of post-event interactions, you position yourself as a catalyst for positive change within your social circles.

Recognize the post-event phase as an ongoing opportunity to contribute to the well-being of those around you. Your commitment to expressing gratitude and fostering meaningful connections serves as a beacon of positivity, creating a ripple effect that extends far beyond the confines of individual events.

In each interaction, whether through a thank-you message or a thoughtful gesture, you are not merely concluding an event but opening doors to deeper understanding and collaboration. View the post-event landscape as a dynamic canvas where you continuously paint strokes of connection, contributing to the masterpiece of intertwined lives.

Immersing yourself in the richness of post-event interactions goes beyond mere etiquette; it becomes a practice of building a supportive and interconnected social ecosystem. Your investment in expressing gratitude and cultivating meaningful connections becomes a cornerstone for lasting relationships.

As you navigate this landscape, consider the reciprocity that blooms when you invest time and energy in others. The joy derived from genuine expressions of gratitude and the cultivation of meaningful connections is a shared experience, creating a tapestry of connections that enrich the collective fabric of your social network.

Embrace the philosophy that the conclusion of an event is not a final chapter but a gateway to continuous growth and understanding.

The shared tapestry of human experience is woven with threads of connection, gratitude, and collaboration. Your role in this tapestry is dynamic, and the post-event phase is where you actively contribute to its evolving narrative.

In summary, the conclusion of an event is not the end but a continuation of a narrative that unfolds through the art of post-event interactions. Mastering this art enriches not only your personal journey but also the collective experience of those around you. As you move forward, approach each post-event engagement as an opportunity to contribute positively, nurture connections, and foster a social landscape characterized by resilience, reciprocity, and enduring relationships.

Chapter Nine

Maintaining and Deepening Relationships

"Depth of friendship does not depend on the length of acquaintance." – Rabindranath Tagore

Regular Communication

Nurturing relationships is an active endeavor that goes beyond intentions. Gain practical insights into staying connected with friends and acquaintances without encroaching on personal space. Recognize the subtle art of reaching out and expressing genuine interest in their lives.

Maintain a nuanced balance between digital and in-person communication. While digital platforms offer convenience, face-to-face interactions provide depth and authenticity. Strive to ensure connections thrive both digitally and in the real world.

Understanding personal boundaries is crucial. Respect the individual needs and limits of friends and acquaintances, fostering an environment of trust. Tailor communication to suit individual dynamics, avoiding a one-size-fits-all approach.

Appreciate the diversity within relationships. Recognize each person's uniqueness and tailor interactions to the nuances of each connection. This personalized approach contributes to the depth and richness of your social tapestry.

Be attuned to the ebb and flow of connection. Adapt to different needs, engaging more actively during challenging moments or celebrations and maintaining a subtle presence when necessary. This adaptability demonstrates emotional intelligence.

Initiate meaningful conversations that delve beyond the surface. Explore shared interests, dreams, and aspirations, fostering a deeper connection. Challenge yourself to discuss profound topics, creating space for vulnerability and authentic expression.

Celebrate the successes and milestones of those in your social circle with genuine enthusiasm. Acknowledge and rejoice in achievements, big or small, strengthening the bonds of connection. Shared joy becomes a cornerstone of positive relationships.

Offer a listening ear and empathetic support in challenging times. Actively engage in conversations that allow the expression of feelings, demonstrating reliability and compassion. Moments of vulnerability forge deeper connections and build trust.

Express gratitude openly and regularly within your social circles. A simple "thank you" affirms the value you place on connections, fostering a positive atmosphere. Express gratitude for shared experiences, acts of kindness, or moments of support.

Incorporate shared activities and rituals into relationships. Create traditions, such as a monthly coffee date or a regular game night, contributing to the fabric of connections. Shared experiences provide stability and a sense of shared history.

Acknowledge individual growth within your social circle. Embrace changes that come with personal development, supporting aspirations, and celebrating milestones. Encouragement contributes to an atmosphere of positivity and mutual empowerment.

Be mindful of your words and actions, creating a safe and welcoming space for open communication. Consider the impact of your choices on relationship dynamics, fostering an environment where everyone feels heard and respected.

Develop a habit of checking in on the well-being of friends and acquaintances. A simple text asking about their day demonstrates genuine concern, creating a foundation of trust and reliability.

Seek opportunities to collaborate and work together on shared goals or projects. Personal or professional collaboration fosters unity and mutual accomplishment, creating a positive association within relationships.

Encourage open communication within social circles. Create a space where everyone feels comfortable expressing their thoughts, feelings, and concerns without fear of judgment. Actively listen, valuing the diversity of experiences and opinions.

Be mindful of the impact of technology on relationships. While digital communication offers convenience, make time for face-to-face interactions. Schedule regular meet-ups, outings, or gatherings to maintain vibrancy beyond the digital realm.

Celebrate the uniqueness of each individual within your social circle. Embrace diversity, appreciating different perspectives, backgrounds, and experiences. Inclusivity creates a rich and dynamic social environment.

Take responsibility for your actions and apologize sincerely when necessary. Genuine apologies demonstrate humility and a commitment to repairing rifts within connections, fostering an environment of forgiveness and growth.

Encourage mutual support within your social circles. Champion the aspirations and endeavors of those around you, providing encouragement and assistance. This supportive atmosphere empowers everyone to pursue their goals with confidence.

Celebrate the diversity of interests within your social circle. Engage in activities and discussions that cater to varied tastes and preferences. Inclusivity ensures everyone feels a sense of belonging, contributing to a well-rounded social environment.

Share moments of vulnerability within relationships. Opening up about personal experiences and challenges creates a space for empathy and understanding. This authenticity deepens bonds, fostering an environment where everyone feels seen and accepted.

Recognize the value of quality over quantity in social interactions. Prioritize investing time and energy into relationships that bring fulfillment and joy. Meaningful connections go beyond surface-level engagements.

Embrace spontaneity within relationships, allowing for unexpected moments of connection and joy. Serendipitous experiences create memorable bonds and contribute to the spontaneity that keeps relationships fresh and exciting.

Promote a culture of generosity within relationships. Small gestures of kindness or larger acts of support create a positive atmosphere of reciprocity, strengthening the bonds of connection.

Respect personal space and autonomy. Recognize individual boundaries and preferences, creating an environment where everyone feels comfortable and valued.

Participate actively in the growth and evolution of your social circle. Be proactive in initiating new experiences, introducing diverse perspectives, and engaging in the overall vibrancy of your connections.

Encourage a culture of laughter and joy. Shared moments of humor foster camaraderie and light-heartedness, enhancing the overall atmosphere of your social circle.

Celebrate cultural and individual milestones. Acknowledge and celebrate birthdays, achievements, and personal milestones, reinforcing the value of each individual within relationships.

Practice active empathy. Seek to understand the perspectives and emotions of those around you, fostering an atmosphere of emotional intimacy and mutual understanding.

Create opportunities for shared learning and growth. Engage in activities or discussions that promote intellectual stimulation and personal development, ensuring social connections remain dynamic.

Encourage open-mindedness. Foster an environment where diverse opinions and ideas are respected, contributing to a rich exchange of perspectives within relationships.

Celebrate the diversity of talents within your social circle. Acknowledge and appreciate unique skills and abilities, enhancing the overall dynamic of your connections.

Foster a culture of resilience. View challenges as opportunities for growth and learning, contributing to the overall strength and durability of social bonds.

Embrace the power of forgiveness. Cultivate an atmosphere of understanding and second chances, allowing for the repair of any fractures within your social circle.

Encourage a culture of gratitude. Express appreciation for the positive contributions of those around you, creating a positive and affirming environment within your social circle.

Cultivate a sense of shared purpose. Foster a community that works towards common goals, aligning efforts towards a shared vision and creating a sense of unity.

Promote a culture of inclusivity. Ensure everyone feels valued and included, celebrating diverse perspectives and backgrounds within your relationships.

Quality Time and Shared Experiences

Diversify your social interactions by incorporating activities that not only strengthen bonds but also deepen connections. Strike a balance between group engagements and one-on-one time, creating a dynamic social landscape that caters to different relationship dynamics. In this chapter, we emphasize the significance of fostering relationships through intentional engagement.

Participate in shared activities that go beyond superficial conversations, ranging from hiking trips to cooking classes. These experiences create lasting memories, forming the foundation for stronger relationships. Tailor shared experiences to individual interests, striking a delicate balance between inclusive group activities and more intimate one-on-one interactions.

Shared laughter during a fun activity acts as a powerful bonding agent, fostering camaraderie. Plan activities that resonate with shared values, ensuring intentional engagement. These shared experiences provide common ground for conversation, making subsequent interactions more natural. Balancing group and individual time prevents relationships from being overwhelmed by too much or too little social interaction.

Meaningful engagement involves active participation and genuine interest in shared experiences. Plan activities that cater to diverse interests within a group to encourage inclusivity and a sense of belonging. The joy of shared achievements, such as completing a project together, strengthens the sense of unity within a group. Engage in a variety of activities to discover common interests not apparent in routine conversations. One-on-one time allows for deeper, more personal conversations, contributing to emotional intimacy.

The challenge of a new experience can create unity and collaboration among participants. Activities involving problem-solving or creativity reveal different strengths and talents within the group. Meaningful engagement is a reciprocal process, with each participant contributing to the shared experience. The memories created through these experiences become the stories that bind individuals together over time. Striking a balance between group dynamics and individual connections ensures everyone feels valued, enriching the tapestry of relationships.

Shared activities break down barriers and facilitate a more natural flow of communication. Inclusivity in planning ensures everyone has the opportunity to contribute ideas and interests. Meaningful engagement involves stepping outside comfort zones, fostering growth individually and collectively. One-on-one time allows for vulnerability and the sharing of personal experiences. Activities aligned with shared goals and aspirations strengthen the sense of purpose within a group, breaking down social barriers.

The diversity of activities ensures inclusivity, and a thoughtful approach to planning considers the preferences and comfort levels of all participants. Shared experiences create a shared language, fostering a unique group identity. Intentional engagement involves being mindful of the needs and expectations of each participant. The balance between group and individual time adapts to evolving relationship dynamics. Activities involving a challenge encourage teamwork and cooperation, with shared accomplishments becoming a source of pride for the group.

Engage in activities that require collaboration to build trust and strengthen bonds within the group. The memories created through shared experiences become a treasure trove carried forward by individuals. Meaningful engagement requires openness to new experiences and a willingness to embrace diversity. Shared activities provide opportunities for spontaneous moments that contribute to a vibrant social landscape. Balancing group interactions and individual connections prevents feelings of exclusion or overwhelm. Activities tapping into participants' passions evoke genuine enthusiasm and joy.

Intentionally plan shared experiences to showcase the value placed on collective connection. One-on-one time allows for a deeper exploration of personal stories and individual perspectives. Meaningful engagement is a journey of discovery, uncovering shared values and common ground. Activities encouraging self-expression foster authenticity within the group. The shared challenges of activities cultivate resilience and adaptability within the group. Striking a balance between planned group activities and spontaneous interactions allows for flexibility. Intentional engagement transforms routine interactions into opportunities for profound connection and growth.

As you incorporate these intentional actions into your social life, consider the transformative impact they can have on your connections. Move beyond routine interactions by infusing variety into your social engagements, ensuring that each experience contributes meaningfully to the tapestry of your relationships.

Explore diverse activities that align with your interests and those of your social circle. Whether it's trying a new hobby together or embarking on a shared adventure, these activities become catalysts for shared joy and discovery. The intentional planning of such experiences showcases your commitment to fostering collective connections.

Value one-on-one time as a space for deeper exploration. Engage in heartfelt conversations that go beyond the surface, allowing individuals to express their thoughts and feelings authentically. Share personal stories and perspectives, creating a foundation of trust and understanding within your relationships. This individualized attention contributes to emotional intimacy, enriching the overall fabric of your social connections.

Meaningful engagement is not only about the activities themselves but also about the collective growth they inspire. Embrace challenges and problem-solving activities that encourage teamwork and cooperation. Shared accomplishments, whether big or small, contribute to a sense of achievement and pride within the group. Celebrate these milestones together, reinforcing the bonds that make your social circle strong.

Ensure inclusivity in your planning process, considering the diverse preferences and comfort levels of all participants. This thoughtful approach fosters a sense of belonging, making everyone feel valued in the group. Break down communication barriers through shared experiences, allowing for a more natural flow of interaction. Inclusivity in planning also encourages everyone to contribute their ideas and interests, creating a collaborative atmosphere.

Step outside your comfort zones collectively, fostering both individual and collective growth. The willingness to embrace new experiences and perspectives strengthens the resilience and adaptability of your social group. Intentionally engaging in activities that align with shared goals reinforces a sense of purpose, providing a meaningful backdrop to your relationships.

These intentional actions go beyond the ordinary, turning routine interactions into opportunities for profound connection and growth. Embrace diversity, be open to spontaneity, and find joy in the shared moments that contribute to a vibrant and fulfilling social landscape. Striking the right balance between group dynamics and individual connections ensures a harmonious and enriched tapestry of relationships.

In your journey of meaningful engagement, cherish the memories created through shared experiences. These moments become the building blocks of a unique and cohesive group identity, strengthening the bonds that tie individuals together. As you continue to navigate this intentional path, may your social connections flourish, and may each interaction be a source of inspiration and joy on your ongoing journey of personal and collective growth.

Handling Conflicts and Misunderstandings

Navigating the inevitable challenges in any relationship requires effective communication strategies rooted in empathy and understanding. To enhance relationship dynamics:

1. Apologize and Forgive with Purpose:

Understand the art of apologizing and forgiving. Recognize these tools as powerful for relationship repair and transformative growth. Apologize not as a sign of weakness but as a demonstration of emotional maturity.

2. Constructive Conflict Approach:

View conflicts as stepping stones toward deeper connections. Cultivate active listening skills to comprehend emotions during disagreements. Use "I" statements to express feelings without blame. Maintain a calm demeanor and explore non-verbal cues for sincere expression.

3. Thoughtful Reactions:

Develop the habit of taking a pause before responding. Allow thoughtful and measured reactions for constructive resolution. Consider conflict resolution as a collaborative effort, emphasizing shared goals and understanding your partner's perspective.

4. Reflective Practices:

Integrate reflective practices into conflict resolution for personal insights. Acknowledge forgiveness as a gift to yourself, releasing the burden of resentment.

5. Apology Languages:

Explore different apology languages, recognizing individual preferences. Foster a culture of forgiveness within relationships, emphasizing its healing power.

6. Learn from Conflicts:

Reflect on conflicts as opportunities for learning. Identify triggers and work collaboratively to mitigate them. Find common ground even in differing opinions.

7. Creative Problem-Solving:

Experiment with creative problem-solving techniques. Encourage open and honest communication about feelings. Learn from patterns during conflicts, identifying triggers and working collaboratively to mitigate them.

8. Conflict Resolution Rituals:

Experiment with conflict resolution rituals for closure and commitment. Recognize conflicts as dynamic, requiring an evolving approach over time.

9. Emotional Safety:

Explore the concept of emotional safety. Foster a culture of accountability where each party takes responsibility for their role in conflicts.

10. Regular Relationship Check-Ins:

Implement regular check-ins to discuss the state of the relationship. Address potential issues before they escalate. Develop a shared language for expressing emotions.

11. Growth Mindset:

Encourage a growth mindset within the relationship. View conflicts as opportunities for mutual evolution. Prioritize self-care during conflicts.

12. Creative Conflict Resolution:

Experiment with conflict resolution through creative mediums. Implement a strategy for de-escalation during heated conflicts.

13. Gratitude in Relationships:

Emphasize the power of gratitude in relationships, even during challenging times.

14. External Stressors and Coping Mechanisms:

Recognize the role of external stressors in conflicts. Develop coping mechanisms to manage their impact.

15. Conflict Resolution Workshops and Seminars:

Explore conflict resolution workshops or seminars as a couple. Experiment with different conflict resolution styles. Prioritize emotional intelligence development.

16. Curiosity and Long-Term Vision:

Foster a mindset of curiosity during conflicts. Consider the long-term vision of the relationship, focusing on shared goals and aspirations.

17. Conflict Resolution through Storytelling:

Explore conflict resolution through storytelling. Share personal narratives to deepen mutual understanding.

18. Maintain Mutual Respect:

Prioritize the maintenance of mutual respect, ensuring that conflicts do not erode the foundation of the relationship.

19. Shared Language for Expressing Boundaries:

Develop a shared language for expressing boundaries during conflicts, fostering an environment of respect and consent.

20. Ongoing Dialogue:

Explore conflict resolution as an ongoing dialogue, recognizing that relationships require continuous effort. Celebrate successful conflict resolutions, reinforcing positive behaviors and encouraging future growth within the relationship.

21. Effective Communication Strategies:

Master effective communication strategies such as mirroring, where you repeat your partner's words to ensure understanding, and paraphrasing to confirm comprehension. Utilize these techniques to create a mutual understanding during discussions.

22. Empathy Building:

Cultivate empathy by putting yourself in your partner's shoes. Practice perspective-taking to understand their feelings and thoughts. This strengthens the emotional connection and promotes a supportive environment.

23. Conflict Journaling:

Introduce conflict journaling as a tool for both partners to express their thoughts independently. Share these entries with each other to gain insights into individual perspectives and collaboratively find solutions.

24. Scheduled Reflection Time:

Designate specific times for reflection on the relationship. This structured approach allows both partners to assess their feelings, expectations, and concerns, fostering a proactive approach to conflict resolution.

25. Mindfulness Practices:

Incorporate mindfulness practices into daily life. Techniques such as meditation and deep breathing can help in managing stress and emotional reactivity during conflicts, promoting a calm and focused approach.

26. Personalized Conflict Resolution Plan:

Develop a personalized conflict resolution plan that outlines specific strategies tailored to your relationship dynamics. Having a customized approach ensures that you address conflicts in a way that aligns with your unique needs.

27. Gratitude Rituals:

Establish gratitude rituals where both partners regularly express appreciation for each other. This practice creates a positive atmosphere and reinforces the value each partner brings to the relationship.

28. Joint Problem-Solving Sessions:

Schedule joint problem-solving sessions where both partners collaboratively address recurring issues. This structured approach allows for a systematic exploration of solutions, encouraging a sense of unity in resolving challenges.

29. Boundary Setting Workshop:

Attend a boundary-setting workshop together to enhance your understanding of personal boundaries and communication styles. This shared experience can lead to improved communication and respect for each other's individual limits.

30. Community Engagement:

Engage with community resources that support healthy relationships. Attend local events, workshops, or support groups focused on relationship dynamics. Connecting with others who share similar goals can provide additional perspectives and insights.

31. Conflict Resolution Retreat:

Consider participating in a conflict resolution retreat as a dedicated time for introspection and shared growth. Retreats offer a structured environment for deepening understanding and acquiring practical skills to navigate conflicts.

32. Relationship Mentorship:

Seek relationship mentorship from a couple with a strong and communicative partnership. Learning from experienced individuals can provide valuable insights and guidance as you navigate the complexities of your own relationship.

33. Couples Therapy:

Explore couples therapy as a proactive measure to strengthen your relationship. Professional guidance can offer tools and strategies tailored to your specific challenges, promoting a healthier connection.

34. Mindful Conflict Escalation:

Develop a mindful conflict escalation plan that includes signals or cues to de-escalate tensions. Establishing clear communication during heated moments helps prevent conflicts from escalating unnecessarily.

35. Weekly Relationship Rituals:

Introduce weekly relationship rituals, such as dedicated date nights or meaningful conversations. Consistent rituals create a sense of stability and reinforce the commitment to nurturing the relationship.

36. Conflict Resolution Book Club:

Form a conflict resolution book club with your partner, reading and discussing literature on effective communication and relationship building. Shared reading experiences provide a platform for open conversations about relationship dynamics.

37. Role Reversal Exercises:

Engage in role reversal exercises during discussions to promote empathy. Take turns expressing each other's perspectives, fostering a deeper understanding of the challenges and viewpoints each partner brings to the relationship.

38. Digital Detox During Conflicts:

Implement a digital detox during conflicts to minimize distractions. Create a dedicated space for face-to-face communication without the interference of electronic devices, fostering a more intimate and focused exchange.

39. Surprise Appreciation Gestures:

Surprise your partner with appreciation gestures during or after conflicts. Small acts of kindness, such as a thoughtful note or a favorite treat, can help diffuse tension and reinforce the positive aspects of your relationship.

40. Shared Vision Board:

Create a shared vision board that visually represents your collective goals and aspirations as a couple. This visual reminder can serve as a motivational tool during conflicts, emphasizing the shared journey you are navigating together.

Chapter Ten

Conclusion

Recap and Encouragement

As the final chapter of "How to be Outgoing: Step-by-Step Strategies to Transform Your Social Life" unfolds, take a moment to reflect on the profound strides you've made. Franklin D. Roosevelt's words resonate: the only barrier to tomorrow has been the doubts of today. Each chapter dismantled those doubts, revealing the latent power within you to embrace a more outgoing and socially enriched life.

Essential lessons unfolded, from understanding outgoing behavior to conquering social anxiety. Each chapter acted as a stepping stone, guiding you toward a more confident, engaging version of yourself. Celebrate your progress; the journey to becoming more outgoing is a series of small victories.

As you continue forward, remember that transformation isn't about perfection but the continual process of growth. Embrace setbacks as opportunities for learning, a testament to your resilience. Now, standing at the crossroads of self-discovery and interpersonal growth, acknowledge the myriad ways your journey has unfolded.

Think of genuine smiles breaking through self-doubt, your introduction paving the way for meaningful connections, and confronting social anxiety with newfound understanding. Visualize your social network expanding as you embrace discomfort, make the first move, and introduce yourself to new faces. Each interaction, small or significant, plays a crucial role in shaping your outgoing self.

Consider the evolving nature of your conversations, from weather talks to engaging dialogues on shared passions. Recall practice exercises that navigated awkward silences, turning potential stumbling blocks into opportunities for deeper connection. Ponder the power dynamics in body language, recognizing how subtle cues influence any interaction.

Reflect on the significant role attire played, understanding how clothing choices signal confidence and authenticity. Delve into the cultural nuances of handshakes, realizing a simple gesture can transcend cultural boundaries. Consider the impact of your online presence, as your engaging profile and thoughtful interactions contribute to the digital extension of your social identity.

Contemplate self-awareness exercises that prompted introspection, leading to a deeper understanding and acceptance of your unique qualities. Reflect on overcoming negative self-talk, replacing it with affirmations that fueled your confidence. Consider the structure of your speeches, once a source of anxiety, now a platform to share your thoughts with assurance.

Ponder strategies in exploring new social settings, easing into unfamiliar territories, and finding comfort in discomfort. Reflect on instances making the first move, approaching new individuals with genuine interest. Consider follow-up strategies nurturing connections, allowing relationships to deepen beyond initial encounters.

Contemplate the delicate balance between maintaining and deepening relationships, recognizing the significance of regular communication. Reflect on quality time spent and shared experiences strengthening bonds. Consider effective conflict resolution strategies, understanding conflicts as opportunities for growth and understanding.

Ponder efforts planning and hosting events, creating inviting atmospheres where connections flourish. Reflect on etiquette at social gatherings, strategies for effective mingling, and graceful exits from conversations. Consider the impact of post-event follow-ups, acknowledging the role of gratitude and acknowledgment in relationship dynamics.

Contemplate the essence of depth in friendships, understanding it transcends the length of acquaintance. Reflect on nuances of regular communication, recognizing boundaries while maintaining meaningful connections. Consider planning activities that strengthen bonds and the importance of shared experiences in fostering deeper connections.

Ponder myriad ways you've utilized online networking and social media, crafting an engaging profile reflecting your personality. Reflect on discussions within online communities, finding relevance and connection in the digital realm. Consider the delicate balance between online and offline interactions, recognizing the symbiotic relationship between the two.

Contemplate the journey through social anxiety, recognizing symptoms and triggers. Reflect on coping mechanisms employed, from breathing techniques to mindfulness practices. Consider seeking professional help as a step toward greater self-awareness and growth, dismantling the stigma associated with seeking support.

Ponder insights gained from planning events, creating environments conducive to positive guest experiences. Reflect on etiquette while attending events, strategies for effective mingling, and graceful exits from conversations. Consider the significance of post-event follow-ups, acknowledging the impact of gratitude and acknowledgment on relationship strength.

Contemplate the evolution of your communication style, recognizing the importance of recognizing and respecting boundaries. Reflect on planning activities that strengthened bonds and the significance of shared experiences in fostering a sense of connection. Consider the effectiveness of conflict resolution strategies, understanding conflicts as opportunities for growth.

Ponder recapitulation of key takeaways, each chapter contributing to your growth as a more outgoing individual. Reflect on encouragement embedded in these pages, urging you to celebrate progress, no matter how incremental. Consider the ongoing process of transformation, recognizing setbacks are not failures but stepping stones to further growth.

Contemplate the courage and resilience displayed throughout this journey, facing challenges head-on and emerging stronger each time. Reflect on encouragement to embrace occasional setbacks as opportunities for learning and refinement. Consider the testament to resilience and acknowledgment of courage in confronting challenges with determination.

Ponder natural progression of your journey standing at the crossroads of a more socially vibrant future. Reflect on the ongoing quest for personal development and resources available to refine your skills and deepen your understanding. Consider suggested readings, online communities, workshops, and professional guidance as avenues for continued growth.

Contemplate continuation of your journey, recognizing next steps involve delving into recommended readings, engaging with like-minded individuals, participating in workshops or online courses, and seeking professional guidance. Reflect on ongoing commitment to personal development, understanding your journey doesn't conclude here; it evolves into a lifelong pursuit of growth and connection.

Consider the impact of each step forward, recognizing you not only enrich your own life but contribute to a more vibrant and interconnected community. Reflect on shared experience of transformation, understanding the journey to being outgoing is not just a personal endeavor; it's a collective narrative that transforms not only individuals but the world they inhabit.

Ponder safe travels on your continuing journey to a more outgoing and socially fulfilled you, understanding each interaction, smile, and connection contributes to the ever-evolving narrative of your life. Reflect on understanding the journey to being outgoing is not just a destination; it's a dynamic and shared experience, shaping not only your individual story but also the collective tapestry of human connection.

Next Steps and Resources

Standing at the crossroads of a more socially vibrant future, envision your journey progressing naturally, augmented by resources awaiting your exploration. As you delve into recommended readings, focus on materials delving into social dynamics and personal growth. Engage actively in like-minded online communities, whether through forums or social media groups dedicated to personal development. Take part in workshops or online courses that specialize in communication skills, confidence-building, and relationship development. For personalized guidance, consider seeking support from professionals such as life coaches or therapists, addressing specific challenges or accelerating your personal growth.

Invest in your personal development continuously to fortify the foundation laid within these pages. Share your experiences with others, seek guidance when needed, and remember that this journey is an ongoing commitment to growth and connection. Each step forward not only enriches your life but contributes to a more vibrant and interconnected community. The journey to being outgoing is not just personal; it transforms not only individuals but the world they inhabit.

As you progress, explore literature that informs and inspires, guiding you through the complexities of human interactions and personal evolution. Tap into the collective wisdom of online communities, fostering a rich environment for shared learning. Immerse yourself in workshops designed to push boundaries, offering hands-on experiences that hone your communication skills and boost confidence. Consider online courses as virtual avenues for growth, allowing you to tailor your learning experience to your pace and preferences. Leverage the expertise of professionals for personalized guidance, unlocking your full potential in navigating social challenges.

Embrace mentorship by seeking individuals who have mastered the art of being outgoing. Attend networking events and conferences to expand your horizons, connecting with industry leaders and enthusiasts passionate about personal development. Establish a routine of self-reflection, dedicating time to assess progress and identify areas for improvement. Journal your thoughts and experiences, creating a tangible record that serves as a source of motivation during challenging times. Foster a growth mindset, viewing setbacks as opportunities for learning and cultivating resilience.

Experiment with new social settings, pushing beyond your comfort zone for personal transformation. Initiate conversations with individuals from diverse backgrounds, embracing the richness that different perspectives bring to your social understanding. Volunteer for community initiatives to contribute to a greater cause and expand your social network meaningfully. Cultivate a habit of active listening, honing your ability to connect with others on a deeper level.

Utilize technology to your advantage, exploring apps and platforms that facilitate skill development and connect you with like-minded individuals. Establish personal goals for your social journey, breaking them down into manageable steps. Create a vision board that visually represents the outgoing and socially fulfilled person you aspire to become, reinforcing your commitment to growth. Share your insights and lessons learned with others, contributing to the collective wisdom of the personal development community. Form accountability partnerships with friends or peers who share similar goals, providing mutual support and encouragement.

Attend personal development retreats to immerse yourself in an environment dedicated to introspection, learning, and transformative experiences. Embrace solitude as a tool for self-discovery, allowing moments of quiet reflection to deepen your understanding of your own desires and aspirations. Experiment with different forms of creative expression, such as writing, art, or music, as outlets for self-discovery and emotional exploration. Practice mindfulness techniques, incorporating meditation and breathing exercises into your daily routine to foster mental clarity and emotional resilience.

Engage in physical activities that promote overall well-being, recognizing the interconnectedness between physical health and social confidence. Join hobby groups or clubs centered on your interests, providing additional opportunities to connect with others who share similar passions. Participate in public speaking events, gradually increasing your comfort level with expressing yourself in front of diverse audiences. Attend cultural events to broaden your horizons, exposing yourself to different perspectives and enhancing your cultural intelligence.

Embrace a spirit of continuous learning, acknowledging that every interaction and experience contributes to your ongoing personal development. Explore virtual reality experiences that simulate social scenarios, allowing you to practice and refine your social skills in a controlled environment. Foster a sense of gratitude for the connections you've made and the lessons learned, recognizing the abundance present in your social journey. Create a support system of friends and family who understand and encourage your commitment to personal growth.

Engage in philanthropic activities, contributing your time and skills to make a positive impact on the lives of others. Develop a repertoire of icebreakers and conversation starters, easing social interactions and making them more enjoyable for all parties involved. Seek out positive role models, individuals whose outgoing nature and social finesse inspire and guide you on your own journey. Incorporate humor into your interactions, recognizing its power to break the ice and create an atmosphere of warmth and connection.

Set boundaries for yourself, ensuring that your social engagements align with your values and contribute positively to your well-being. Create a "comfort zone expansion" plan, gradually exposing yourself to increasingly challenging social situations. Identify and challenge limiting beliefs that may hinder your progress, replacing them with affirmations that foster a positive mindset. Invest time in nature, recognizing its restorative qualities and its ability to enhance your overall sense of well-being. Develop a habit of constructive self-talk, cultivating a positive inner dialogue that supports and encourages your outgoing journey.

Embrace the concept of lifelong learning, recognizing that each day brings new opportunities for personal and social growth. Document your personal victories, celebrating even the smallest achievements on your path to becoming more outgoing.

Attend personal development seminars led by renowned experts in the field, absorbing their insights and strategies for social transformation. Establish a routine of self-care, prioritizing activities that nourish your mind, body, and spirit for sustained social well-being. Explore diverse cuisines and dining experiences, using them as opportunities to connect with others over shared meals. Volunteer as a mentor for individuals who may be navigating their own journeys to increased social confidence.

Experiment with mindfulness-based practices, such as mindful walking or mindful eating, to enhance your present-moment awareness. Incorporate acts of kindness into your daily routine, recognizing the positive impact they can have on your social interactions. Celebrate cultural diversity, seeking out opportunities to engage with individuals from different backgrounds and perspectives. Reflect on the interconnectedness of your social journey with broader societal transformations, understanding the ripple effect of positive social interactions on a global scale.

Made in United States
Troutdale, OR
07/17/2024